Movement, Structure and the

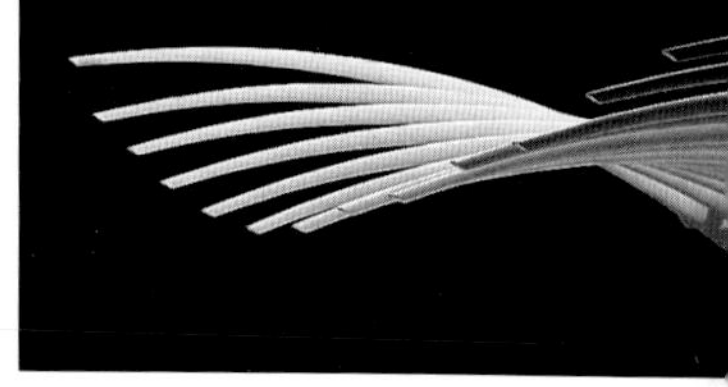

Movement, Structure

Work of Santiago Calatrava

ALEXANDER TZONIS
LIANE LEFAIVRE

and the Work of Santiago Calatrava

BIRKHÄUSER
BASEL·BOSTON·BERLIN

Library of Congress
Cataloging-in-Publication Data

A CIP catalogue record for this
book is available from the
Library of Congress,
Washington D.C., USA

Deutsche Bibliothek
Cataloging-in-Publication Data

Tzonis, Alexander:
Movement, Structure and the Work
of Santiago Calatrava/
Alexander Tzonis; Liane Lefaivre. -
Orig. -Ausg. -Basel;
Boston; Berlin: Birkhäuser 1995
ISBN 3-7643-5050-4
NE: Lefaivre, Liane; Calatrava,
Santiago [Ill.]

Design QUIM NOLLA, Barcelona

Illustrations:
Archive Santiago Calatrava, Zurich
Archive Alexander Tzonis-Liane Lefaivre, Delft

P.O. Box 133, CH-4010 Basel,
Switzerland.

Production: [di´zain]
Editorial Productions,
Barcelona

Printed in Spain

ISBN 3-7643-5050-4
ISBN 0-8176-5050-4
987654321

Contents

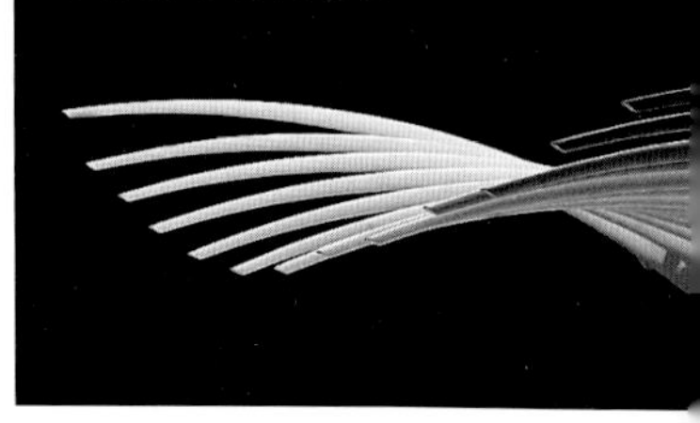

ACKNOWLEDGEMENTS:

WE GRATEFULLY ACKNOWLEDGE THE
ASSISTANCE OF
ANTHONY TISCHHAUSER
AND
KIM MARANGONI,
TOGETHER WITH THE STAFF AT
BIRKHÄUSER
IN BASLE,
OUR COLLABORATOR
QUIM NOLLA
AND LAST BUT NOT LEAST
TINA AND **SANTIAGO**
CALATRAVA.

WE WOULD ALSO LIKE TO EXTEND
A WARM THANKS TO
JOOP DOORMAN,
SPYROS POLLALIS,
DANIEL SCHODEK,
JOHN HEINZ,
TALMA LEVIN,
MICHAEL LEVIN,
TO ALL MEMBERS OF
THE DESIGN KNOWLEDGE SYSTEMS
RESEARCH GROUP,
AND IN PARTICULAR
HENK DE GROOT.

Structure and Wonder

EVERY structure, whether large or small, is a source of wonder. A structure will at first appear miraculous — a "thauma" as Aristotle called it in Mechanika, his treatise on mechanical problems. If no immediate understanding should emerge, that structure will transform itself into a question — an "aporoumenon", according to Aristotle[1] — about its origins and make-up. How did the structure come about? What makes it the way it is? Such wonder is the beginning of excitement, of a search, of thinking about an answer.

BUT with that answer, the feeling of wonder may turn into "Wonder en is gheen wonder" ("A miracle and not a miracle"), to quote the 16th century Dutch engineer Simon Stevin. It was Stevin, who, in this elliptical motto, expressed what happens once a problem is solved. Once there is an explanation, wonder necessarily gives way to disappointment. "We discover that what once appeared to us as wonderful, is no longer wonderful," to quote Ernst Mach, and "our puzzle then turns out to be a puzzle no more ... and takes its place among the shadows of history."[2]

UNLESS, of course, the answer gives rise to another question, and a new wonder — a new search; the mind's eye, looking once more into the structure, will, with each new question, envisage a new answer. "Quid tum?" "What now?" — the motto of Leon Battista Alberti, the great Renaissance architect, theoretician, novelist and engineer. Alberti's "Quid tum?" was associated with the emblem of the winged eye, a most appropriate symbol of the mind's never-ending process of learning, problem solving and dream-work: the transformation, in fact, from "no wonder" into "wonder".

1. Aristotle, MEKANIKA *(Mechanical Problems)*, in: Minor Works, Cambridge and London 1980, p. 331.
2. From the title page of Simon Stevin, *Hypomnemata Mathematica*, (Leyden, 1605). See Ernst Mach, Science of Mathematics, Lassalle, Open Court, 1989 (1893), p. 41.

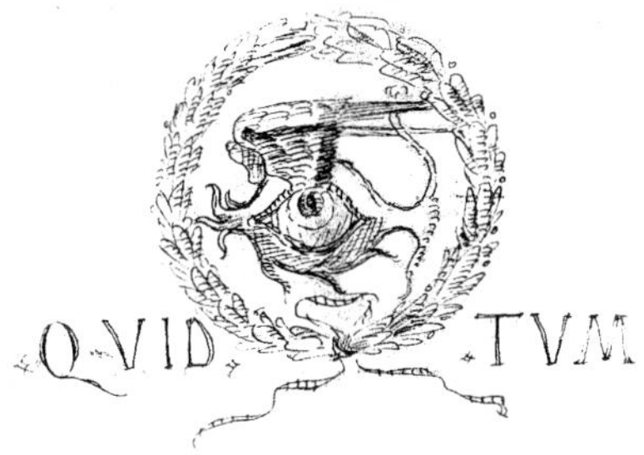

Winged eye, with the motto "Quid Tum". Attributed to L. B. Alberti. From his manuscript of Della famiglia. Florence. Biblioteca Nazionale. cod. II. IV. 38.

Title page from Simon Stevin's Hypomnemata Mathematica, Leyden. 1605.

MOVEMENT is the last thing we tend to associate with structures. Intuition tells us that structures are stationary. They give us the impression of solidity, of being able to resist forces, and channel loads to the ground. We do not expect a structure to change shape, break loose, crack , rupture, snap, come apart or overturn — least of all collapse. Any well-formed structure will, by definition, appear impervious to assaults by wayward forces, or episodes of distress. The very idea of a structure is synonymous with stability, stasis and the rigid organisation of elements in space.

AN ELEMENTARY branch of the science of structures, known as statics, actually ignores movement. Statics conceives well-formed structures as systems of balanced forces — and forces produce movement. By providing counteracting forces, however, structures neutralise this movement, and so induce a state of static equilibrium. Based on this assumption, it is possible to concentrate effectively on specific phenomena, and design an impressive number of simple but nevertheless extremely practical structures, while at the same time accomplishing a few technological feats.

OF COURSE, structures are never at rest; the more knowledge that we acquire about the behaviour of structures, the more we realise how indispensable movement is within them. Although apparently immobile, under closer scrutiny all structures, both artificial and natural, prove to be in state of constant motion. Buildings, bridges, sculpture, trees and even mountains —

3. Heinrich Wölfflin, *Renaissance and Baroque*, London 1964. (First published in German 1888). See in particular the chapter devoted to movement, pp. 58-70.
4. Santiago Calatrava, *Zur Faltbarkeit von Fachwerken. (On the Foldability of Frames)*, Ph. D. Dissertation 1981.

all are constantly being deformed, flexed, stretched and squeezed. They slide and roll. They bend and bow. They sway, tremble, and shudder. Such movement is as a rule imperceptible and momentary, and leaves the overall stability and permanence of the body of the structure undisturbed.

BUT there are other ways in which structure and movement come together, with stability proving to be merely a means towards higher functional goals. As a rule, these goals will concern the accommodation of the movement of people and vehicles. Indeed, structures themselves are subject to movement, from the moment of their erection to the moment of their demolition; in the interim, they may be subject to change.

THROUGHOUT history, movement has frequently emerged as a major symbolic preoccupation. Heinrich Wölfflin showed that the late Renaissance and Baroque periods were particularly obsessed with the significance of the concept of movement. In his famous essay *Renaissance and Baroque,* Wölfflin identified movement as being represented by architectural features which, in relation to the integral forms of classical architecture canon, were "hybrid". Classified among these hybrids were the "immured columns" in the colonnade of Michelangelo's Palazzo dei Conservatori, and the "pushed columns" in his Laurentian Library: "... herm-like pilasters that become wider as they move upwards..." in the juxtaposition of contrasting concave and convex volumes. Such "motifs," as Wölfflin called them, gave the "impression of constant movement ...an unceasing, restless struggle for liberty" achieving the "expression of a directed movement" through the display of "the functions of lifting and carrying ...violent and passionate effort" and, ultimately, the expression of a "wild desire for movement"[3].

WÖLFFLIN'S analysis inspired generations of art historians as they attempted to identify other periods associated with movement as a design strategy, such as

Siegfried Giedion in his *Space, Time and Architecture*. Nevertheless, Wölfflin's ideas, stimulating as they were, had their shortcomings. Not only did his discussions overinterpret a period, they also fell short of linking movement with structural aspects of man-made products. As we have seen, Wölfflin spoke of structural elements, such as columns, but there is very little explanation of why these specific architectural "motifs" expressed the idea of movement. Related to structures, movement has symbolic implications. However, these implications are constrained by the material properties not only of movement, but also of structures — even when their symbolic expression is the product of dream-work, as we shall see.

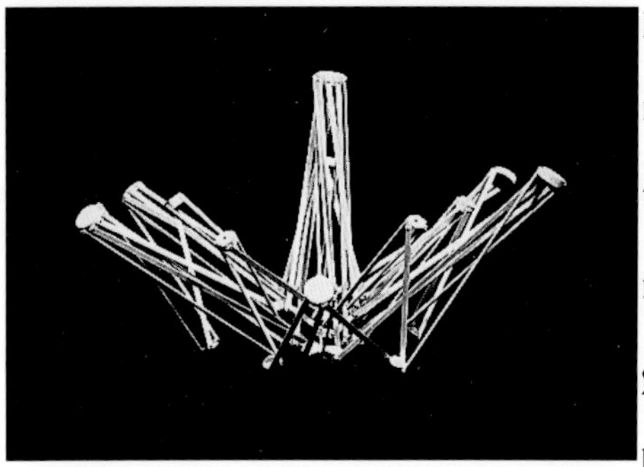
Illustration of a folding structure from Santiago Calatrava's Zur Faltbarkeit von Fachwerken. Ph. Dissertation. 1981.

IN 20th century design culture, movement has, more than ever before, become a fact of life. In view of the importance of unprecedented speed and the impact of global mobility and change on our own lives, this is hardly surprising. The incorporation of movement into structures has become the preoccupation of many designers; this is probably nowhere more apparent than in the work of Santiago Calatrava.

FROM his first, tentative adolescent sketches, either explicitly or implicitly, Calatrava has explored the ways in which structures accommodate movement. Movement was the basis of his Ph.D. thesis *On the Foldability of Frames*[4] at the Swiss Federal Institute of Technology, in Zurich, which examined structures that could be packed and unpacked by means of an ingenious system of compact, movable components. Indeed, we accept that movement is the main theme of his current work: his buildings have sections that unfold, rise up and revolve. His most characteristic structures, namely stations and bridges, are programmatically devoted to movement. The forms of his buildings; infrastructure facilities; sculptures; furniture; utensils; drawings — all are related to some aspect of movement.

THE Calatrava projects examined here are for the most part aimed either at serving circulation needs or fulfilling requirements through the use of mobile elements. If not actually technological feats, almost all are technically complex projects which offer unique answers to the ways in which movement can shape structures. In order to resolve the conflicts stemming from the complex nature of their program, most require careful analysis. Within the same works, these structures also appear to underline the presence of a paradox: striving for permanence in space while generating permanence in time, and achieving it through movement; incorporating fleeting moments within their static body; effacing their own fetishist aura by constantly reminding the viewer of their generic process; manifesting their victory over collapse by pretending to be in the process of falling.

THERE are, in fact, two intertwined themes, both concerned with movement as an ever-evolving poetic device: the broad and evolving preoccupation with history on the one hand, and on the other, the work of Santiago Calatrava.

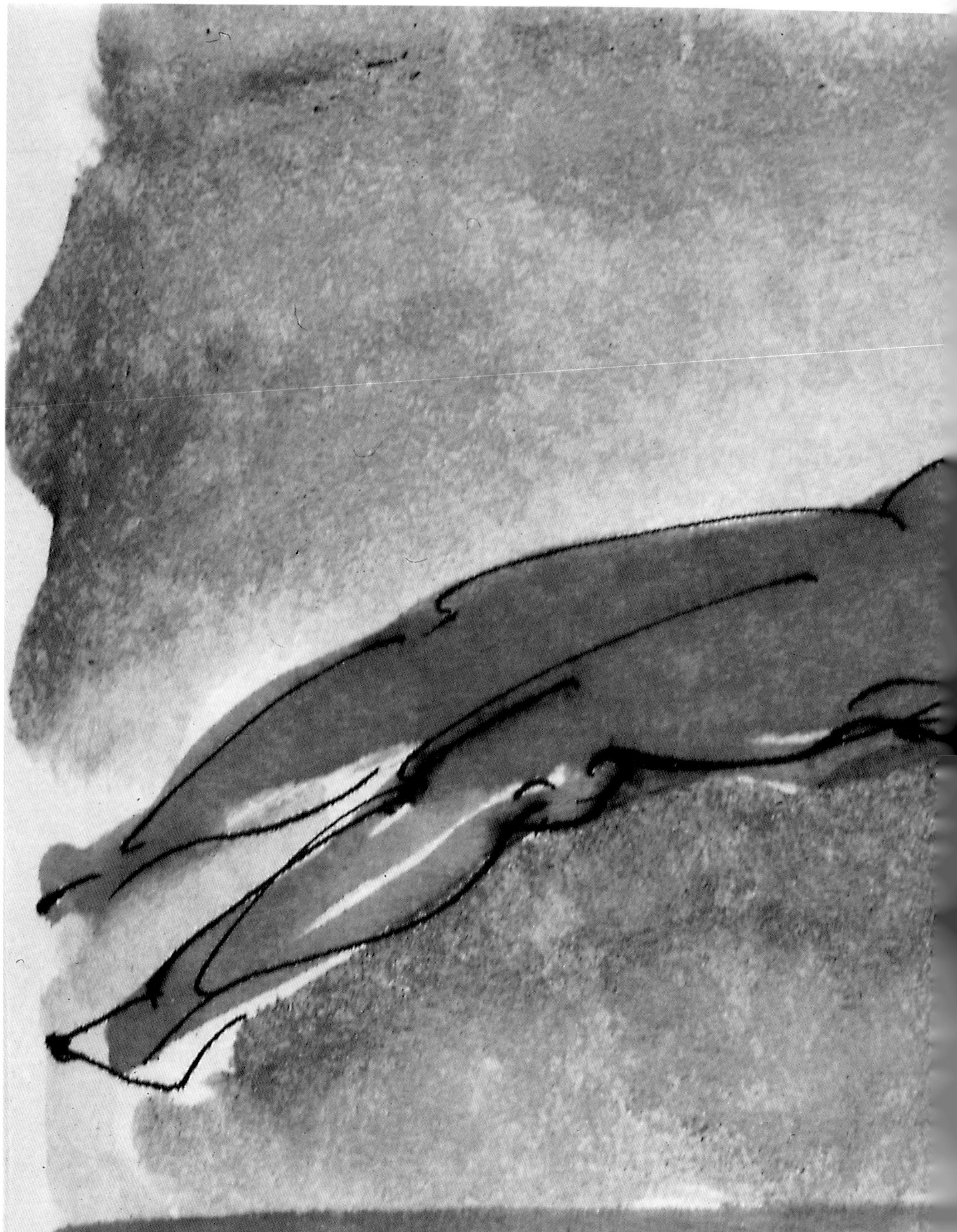

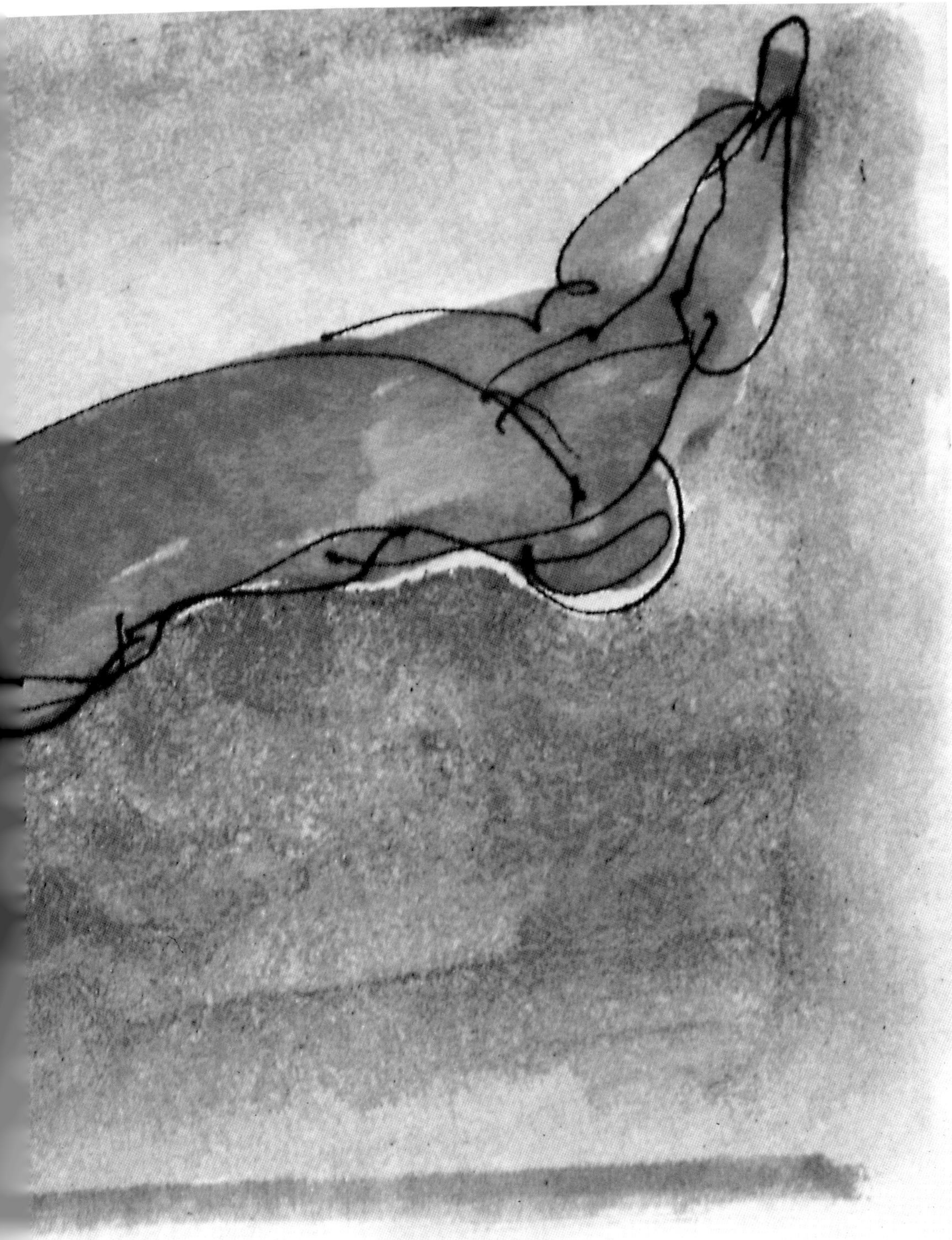

Dream-Work and Moving Structures

THE dream of capturing movement within structures is at least as old as the Bible: "A pillar of cloud ... descended and stood at the tabernacle door" in front of Moses (Exodus, chapter 33) — a movement which can be considered the origin of the spiral form of the Salomonic order.

LESS astonishing, and closer to an engineer's vision, are the contraptions conceived between the 3rd and 1st century BC by Ktesibios of Alexandria, Philo of Byzantium and Hero of Alexandria as moving parts of the design of buildings in Hellenistic times. The most intriguing description of such a mobile artifact is probably Hero's door for a temple: a pneumatic apparatus opens and closes the door and is timed to function in accordance with the scheduling of certain rituals. Hero also describes a mechanical theatre, consisting entirely of automata with moving doors and moving puppet actors carrying out a multiplicity of complicated tasks such as dancing, grouping, sawing or producing sounds — with the audience clueless about what actually caused these movements[5].

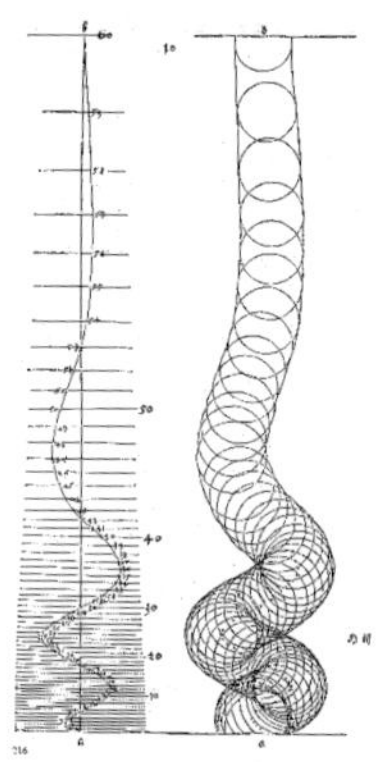

Contour of twisted column. Albrecht Dürer. Underweisung der Messung... 1525. p. 216.

STRUCTURES that move are also a major concern in Vitruvius' treatise "De Architectura" (25 - 23 BC). Along with "Building" and "Clockmaking", "Mechanics" — the designing of machines endowed with "kinesis" (movement) — is in fact identified as one of the three areas which make up the knowledge and activities of an architect. In his tenth book, Vitruvius discusses in

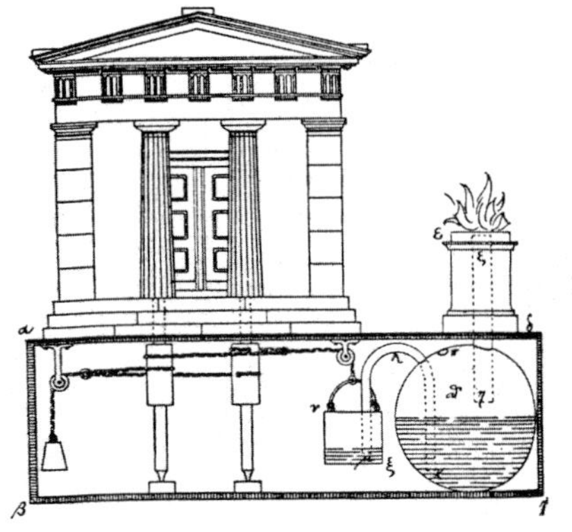

Hero of Alexandria´s pneumatic temple door opener. From Friedrich Klemm. A History of Modern Technology. Cambridge. MIT Press. 1964.

Hero of Alexandria´s Automatic Theater. The Dance of the Bacchantes. From Friedrich Klemm. A History of Modern Technology. Cambridge. MIT Press. 1964.

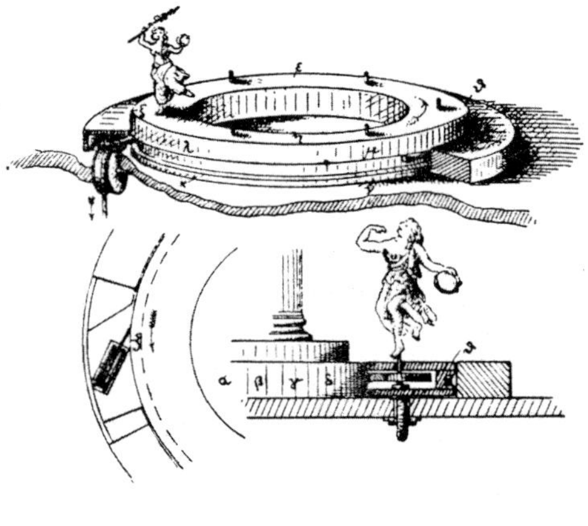

great detail the kinds of machines that are possible, and how they are made. He lists hoisting machines, engines for raising water, water wheels, water mills, the water screw and other types of pump, the water organ and instruments for measuring travelled distances. Of interest to us are the warfare, and specifically the siege machines that he describes — catapults; scorpions; ballistae; the tortoise. The size of these fantastic mobile structures was immense[6].

MOVING structures make their reappearance in a literary genre, referred to as The Mirabilia, dating from the 10th century, and become prominent in Europe from the 12th to the end of the 14th century. True to their title, these writings recount fabulous tales that occur in strange, foreign, far away places. The Mirabilia contain many descriptions of buildings that are astonishing because of their size, their ornamentation and their craftsmanship. The marvelous feature of these buildings is that they are sometimes endowed with movement. In one palace, there is a hall that showers visitors with gifts, while another greets them with a hail of arrows. One entire castle twirls in the wind. In another, only the great hall rotates[7].

MOVEMENT continues to play a highly significant role in Renaissance structures. From the fantastic sounding automata and mobile structures described by Giovanni Fontana in Liber Instrumentorum in the early 15th century — obscure and fascinating though they may be — it is difficult to judge just which are the product of sheer fantasy, the result of experimentation and testing, have a specific function or are simply intended to amaze[8].

5. See Friedrich Klemm, *A History of Modern Technology*, Cambridge 1964, pp. 31 - 36.
6. Marcus Vitruvius Pollio, *De Architectura*, Cambridge 1931, 2 vols.
7. For further reading on the tradition of the architectural mirabilia: see Jacques Le Goff, „Le merveilleux dans l'Occident medieval". In: *L'Imaginaire médieval*, Paris 1985.
8. Giovanni Fontana, *Le macchine cifrate de Giovanni Fontana*, edited by Eugenio Battisti and Giuseppina Saccaro, Milan 1984.
9. See Marcello Fagiolo, *Natura e artificio, l'ordine rustico, le fontane, gli automi nella cultura del manierismo europea*, Rome 1979.

ASTOUNDING mobile structures, machines, instruments of spectacle and pleasure devoid of any productive objective (but also stripped of deeper magical or religious connotations) appear massively during the sixteenth and seventeenth centuries. During the period, they play a major role both in garden and urban settings, and are perhaps more significant than static structures, buildings or sculptures. They become an essential part of public ceremonies and feasts, where entertainment and political indoctrination are blurred into one single hallucinatory happening. The key structures in these events are no longer static. What is admired in these kinetic structures is not scale, or the mastering of space and stability, or the ingenious distribution and control of materials achieving optimal equilibrium; it is movement. Actual, overt, exaggerated movement — not only of the solid members, wheels, doors, columns, figures and simulations of artificial animals dreamed of or attempted throughout antiquity, the middle ages and the beginning of the Renaissance but, more importantly, of unstable materials: water; burning gases; exploding particles[9].

THERE is an abundance of documents and a booming industry of books that describe and analyse designs for water movement — "water structures" — dating from the 17th and 18th centuries. Many of these texts contain long lists of 'mobiles', of which water is the key material: artificial water sources; streams; cataracts; spouts; jets. This same period also witnessed an explosion of lavishly illustrated writings on pyrotechnics, sky rockets, sparklers, smoke screens and polychromatic emissions, as well as torch lights with carefully controlled flames for producing a variety of flashes and other pyrotechnic effects.

SINCE the 17th century, very few architects have felt inclined to incorporate movement into their structures in this literal way. Calatrava's early and deep commitment to the problems of movement make him an exception; as an engineering student at Zurich's Federal Institute of Technology, his Ph.D. thesis closely examined the theme of moving structures.

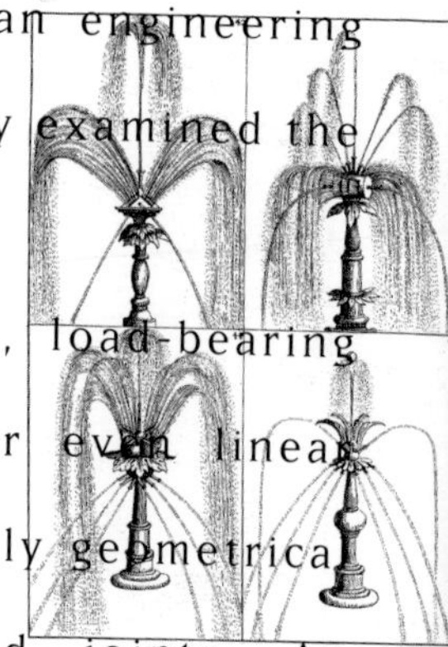

THE subject of Calatrava's thesis was the design of stable, trussed, load-bearing structures that, through folding, could be transformed into planar or even linear structures. In order to realise such a transformation, in addition to purely geometrical considerations, the structures demanded articulation into bars and joints. An investigation into these joints compelled Calatrava to seek advice beyond the architectural and civil engineering departments, and venture into the world of mechanical engineering, when structures move like machines in space, capable of transformation from a packaged to a three-dimensional truss format. (Because of the particular interest of this thesis — which examines the kinetic aspects of structures alongside their geometry, in order to relate the structural properties of their design to the degrees of freedom involved in their compaction — we have provided extensive extracts in the Appendix). This mechanical "initiation" has left its mark on the career of Santiago Calatrava; ever since, he has seen structures as kinetic systems, even when "folding" is not an issue.

EVEN when they move, Calatrava's structures are not just machines. Even when they possess a clear utilitarian value and a functional purpose, the result of rigorous problem-solving procedures — both as design products

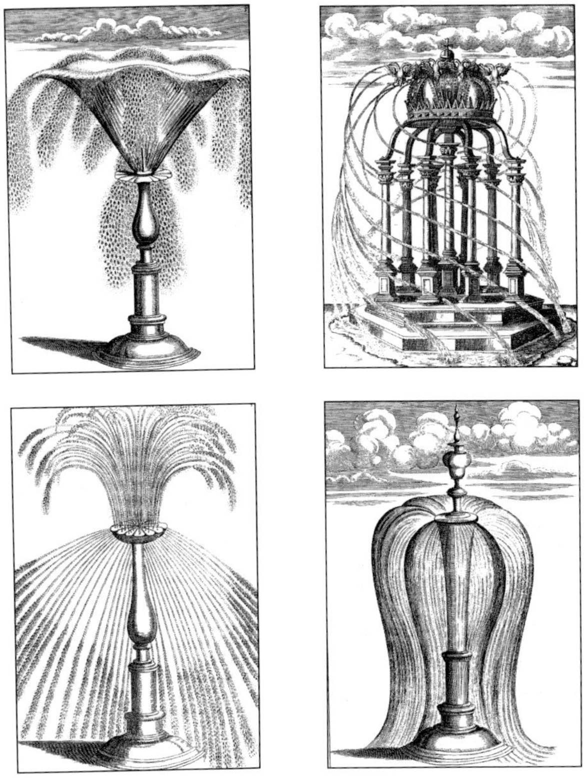

Fountains from Joseph Furtembach.
Architectura recreationis. 1640.

Jean Le Paultre. Recueil general
du Chasteau de Versailles. 1677.

and design processes — they come much closer to the objects found in Leon Battista Alberti's Hypnerotomachia Poliphili[10]. They are dream-works, and as dream-works, they have a "syntax" all their own, based on the dismantling and recombination of things — referred to by Freud as condensation and displacement — to create new "composite structures". It is not surprising that many surrealists were fascinated in this work.[11]

IN the Hypnerotomachia Poliphili, a text only recently attributed to Alberti and written about 25 years after his architectural treatise, structures appear to behave as humans; they are anthropomorphic, not only in their form but frequently in their operation and performance, too. Made up of kinetic elements, they open and close, heave and shudder, all within the framework of a dream that permits them to be both artifacts and animate, corporeal entities.

Illustration of a wind-powered mechanical figure that twirls at every turn of the breeze from the top of a high building. From Hypnerotomachia Poliphili (Venice, 1499).

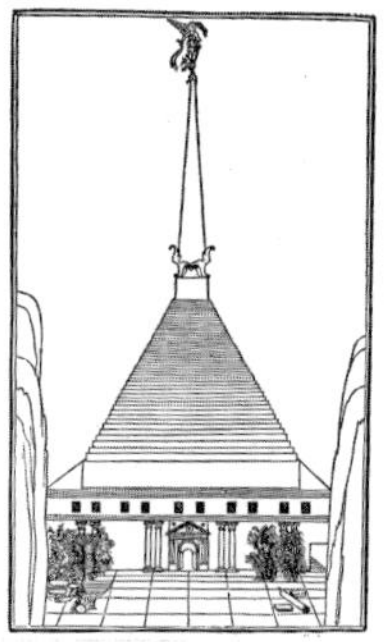

IN 1936, the year when New York was "practically crawling with Surrealist exhibitions", Lewis Mumford wrote in "Surrealism and Civilisation" about the Museum of Modern Art's Surrealist show, stating that the works exhibited seemed to well up from the "willing, wishing, urging, passionate part of man's life" that had been "slighted, stifled and even banished altogether, in favour of practical routines"[12]. It is precisely in this "passionate part of a man's life" that the surrealistic quality of Calatrava's work resides.

THE images that the moving structures of Calatrava invoke seem to well up out of the unconscious, to tap

THE IMAGES THAT THE MOVING STRUCTURES OF CALATRAVA INVOKE SEEM TO WELL UP OUT OF THE UNCONSCIOUS, TO TAP THAT YEARNING, WILLING, INDEED PASSIONATE PART OF LIFE THAT TENDS TO BE SLIGHTED BY PURELY UTILITARIAN AND FUNCTIONAL, AS WELL AS FORMALIST WORKS.

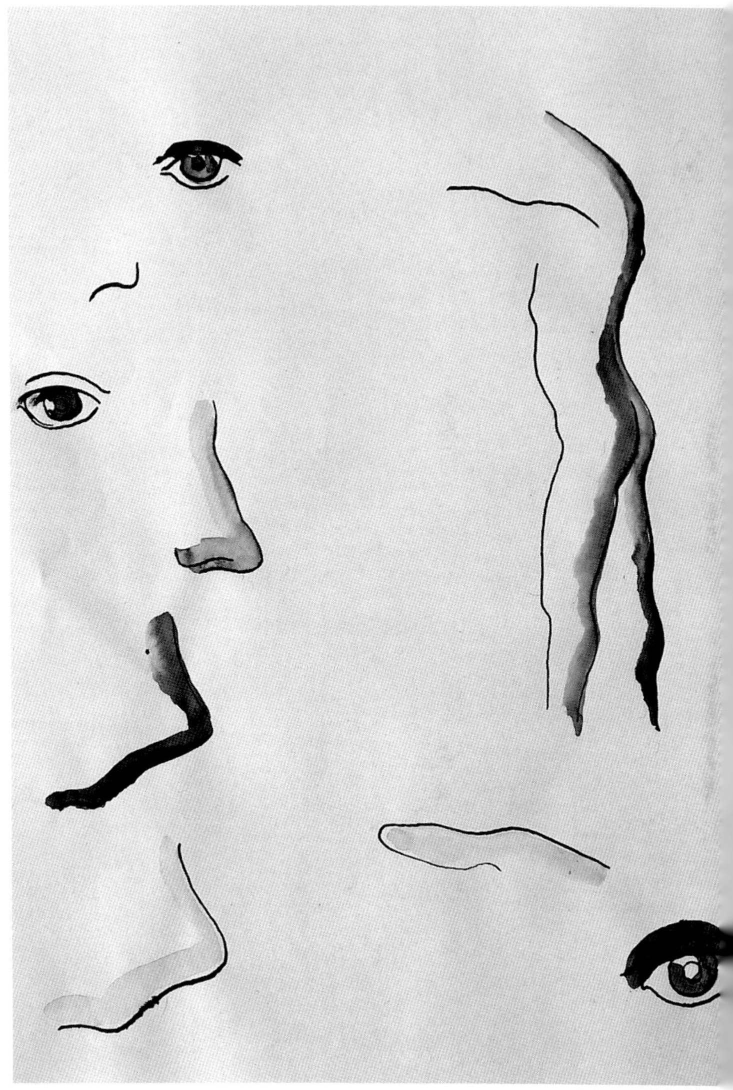

Paintings by Santiago Calatrava. Untitled. From sketchbook (1993) and October-November 1994.

that yearning, willing, indeed passionate part of life that tends to be slighted by purely utilitarian and functional, as well as formalist works. However, as opposed to most Surrealist works, with Calatrava, dream-work is never in conflict with the reality principle and the ego. The liberating power of the imagination is reasserted and restored, but is nevertheless placed at the service of functionality to the same degree as utilitarian engineering is placed at the service of dream-work. Accordingly, our minds are allowed to envision a possible, multifaceted world.

SWIMMING pools, for example, are not usually mobile; nor do they float in the air. Nevertheless, in a very early project — completed with fellow students at the Federal Institute of Technology in Zurich — the 26 year old Calatrava designed a transparent, doughnut shaped, mobile swimming pool made of plastic sheeting 1 millimetre thick and holding 20,000 litres of water, suspended by cables from the ceiling of the building[13].

A MORE subdued although deeply oniric example of displacement and condensation is the way in which movement was incorporated into the Ernsting Warehouse and Distribution Centre in Coesfeld, Westfalen. Working with codesigners Bruno Reichlin and Fabio Reinhart, the project gave Calatrava his first opportunity to design a mobile element as part of a structure, and to thus combine functional requirements with the poetics of movement.

10. Leon Battista Alberti, *De re aedificatoria*; latin text and translation into Italian by Giovanni Orlandi. Milan, Polifilo, 1966. See also the english translation, *On the Art of Building*, by Joseph Rykwert, Neal Leach and Robert Tavenor, Cambridge 1988. *The Hypnerotomachia Poliphili*, first published in Venice at the press of Aldus Manutius in 1499, has been reprinted by Garland, New York 1976. See also Liane Lefaivre, *Leon Battista Alberti's Hypnerotomachia Poliphili*, forthcoming.

11. See Sigmund Freud, The *Interpretation of Dreams*, Standard Edition of the Complete Works of Sigmund Freud, translated by James Strachey, London 1959.

12. Lewis Mumford, *Surrealism and Civilization*, in: New Yorker, Dec. 19, 1936.

13. The official Title was *Plastisches Gestalten*, it was the project for a Sculpture in the cupola of the Federal Institute of Technology in Zurich, co-authored by Brigitte Allensbach, Jürg Altherr, Markus Bischofsberger, Orlando Cagnoni, Christoph Haerle, Sabine Habacher, Hans Hugi, Hans Hürlimann, Toni Ruegge, Peter Schindler, Cécile Wick, Erick Wyler.

Suspended pool in the hall of the Federal Institute of Technology in Zurich. Scetchbook 1979.

A TRANSPARENT, DOUGHNUT SHAPED, MOBILE SWIMMING POOL MADE OF PLASTIC SHEETING 1 MILLIMETRE THICK AND HOLD-ING 20,000 LITRES OF WATER, SUSPENDED BY CABLES FROM THE CEILING OF THE BUILDING.

Dream-Work and Moving Structures

Calatrava. Sculpture. Untitled. 1993.

Nike figure From the frieze of the Athena Nike Temple, Acropolis Museum, Athens. 409 BC.

WHEN THE DOORS ARE OPENED BY MEANS OF A FRAME HIDDEN BEHIND THIS "KNEE", THE SLATS PROTRUDE FORWARDS TO PROVIDE A KIND OF PROTECTIVE CANOPY OVER THE ENTRANCE.

Ernstings Warehouse

Dream-Work and Moving Structures

Ernstings Warehouse

The garage doors at Ernsting's Warehouse and Distribution Centre. Coesfeld.

Ernstings Warehouse

Dream-Work and Moving Structur

Curtain wall. Ernsting's.

Ernstings Warehouse

THE commission was to design three garage doors for the west façade, and dress a structure which had already been built. Calatrava, Reichlin and Reinhart used the opportunity to investigate questions of design that concern the relationship between movement and structures, and more specifically, the problem of moving the sections of a structure. Each of the doors rise and fall through the displacement of a series of aligned alumium slats, articulated in the centre like a knee. When the doors are opened by means of a frame hidden behind this "knee", the slats protrude forwards to provide a kind of protective canopy over the entrance. The canopy's swooping line is due to the gradual and uniform change of the position of articulation along the series of slats: lower at the sides, higher towards the centre — a simple, functional and wholly original solution (designed and patented by Calatrava).

THERE is another dimension to this motion: the relationship between textiles and architecture — a reflection, one might say, of Semper's hypothesis that the principle of dressing, or "Bekleidung", is the true essence of architecture[14]. According to Semper, woven textiles were the original definers of architectural space. In the design of the garage doors and the cladding of the side walls of Ernsting — ironically, itself a textile firm — the Semperian hypothesis assumes a dream-like, delusional interpretation, free of the "censorship" of conventional architectural common sense. For example, with the garage doors closed, the "drapery" that covers them appears to hang straight. When they lift, the "knee" joints bend and the "cloth" will correspondingly fold. The

14. Gottfried Semper, „Style: the Textile Art", in *The Four Elements of architecture and Other Writings*, translated by Harry Francis Mallgrave and Wolfgang Herrmann, Cambridge, 1989, pp. 254ff.

Detail of the knee from the Nike Figure from the Athena Nike Temple.

image of cloth is taken to an equally playful extreme on the sides of the building, where the curtain wall seems to flutter in the breeze. Evidently, this image of a fluttering curtain is a source of fascination to Calatrava — he brings it to life again in his 1993 kinetic sculpture, entitled "S42".

FLYING, a typical theme of dreams, is encountered in two kinetic, wing-like structures by Calatrava, both of which are constructed in concrete: the Concrete Pavilion — the so-called "shadow machine" — for the 1989 Swissbau in Basle, and the similar piece exhibited by Calatrava in 1993 at the Museum of Modern Art in New York. No matter how often we experience their slow, perpetual, hypnotic movement emanating from the more simple movement of each individual element, they impart a strange feeling that, as their hidden motor drives them, they are alive. In the Concrete Pavilion in Basle, the oniric effect is enhanced by modulating the illumination of the sculpture, to cast shadows of the members on the floor and on the wall. But it is also derived from the strangeness of using concrete as the material for mobile members. Concrete, categorised in the minds of most people as a hard and heavy material, suddenly appears with the light and graceful movement of the wings of a large bird, the body of a dolphin or the hands of a skillful dancer.

THE dream-like effect is also produced by the aimlessness with which the structures seem to move. There is, in fact, a deeper purpose: the works were explicitly aimed at a demonstration of the possibilities of concrete that went beyond the qualities that most people habitually associate with a rough, stern, heavy, steadfast and rock-like material, usually applied to solid, sturdy products. Although less overtly stated, the second sculpture, a mobile structure also of concrete, had the same objective. Metal, wood, and more recently some plastics, are normally used in machine construction. They are

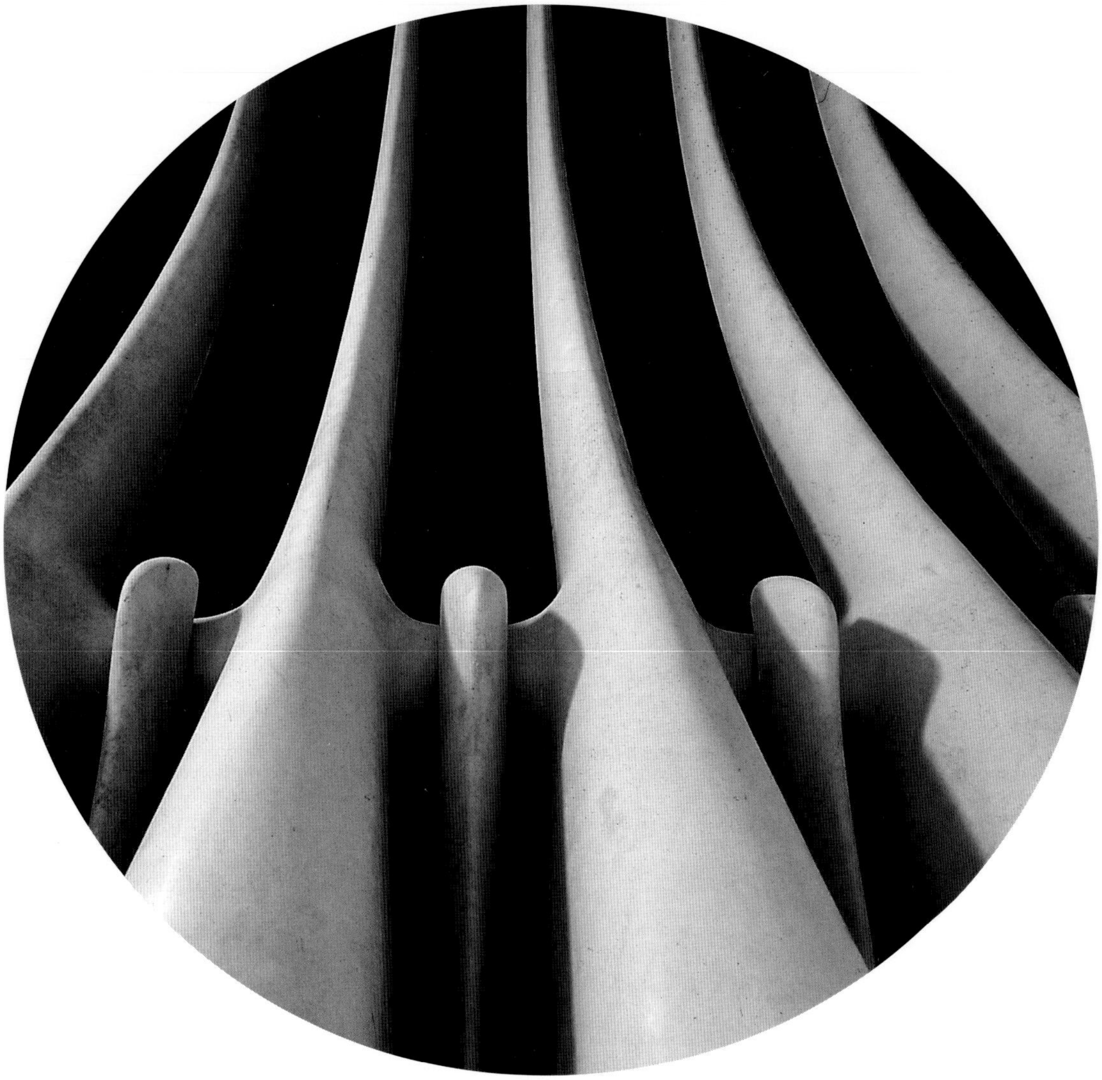

Swissbau Concrete Pavilion

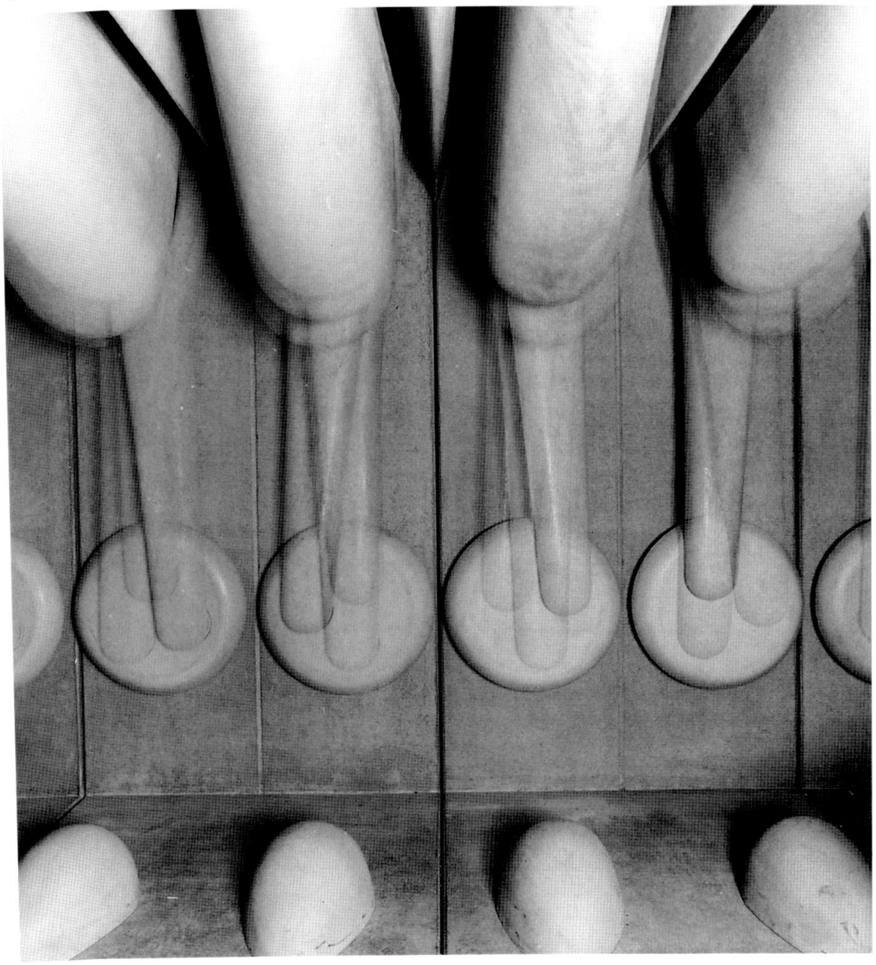

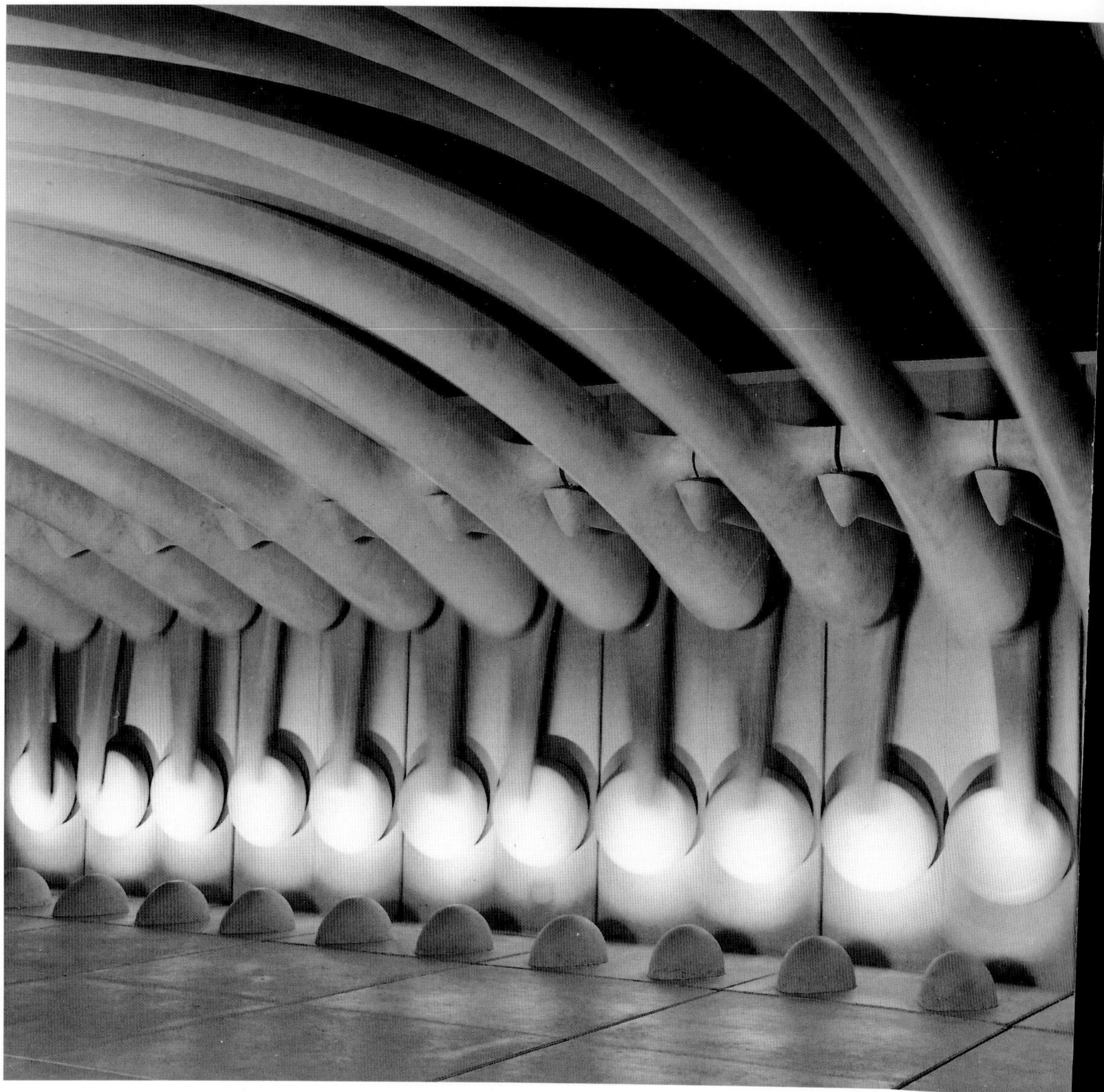

Dream-Work and Moving Structures
Swissbau Concrete Pavilion

Kinetic sculpture at the Museum of Modern Art

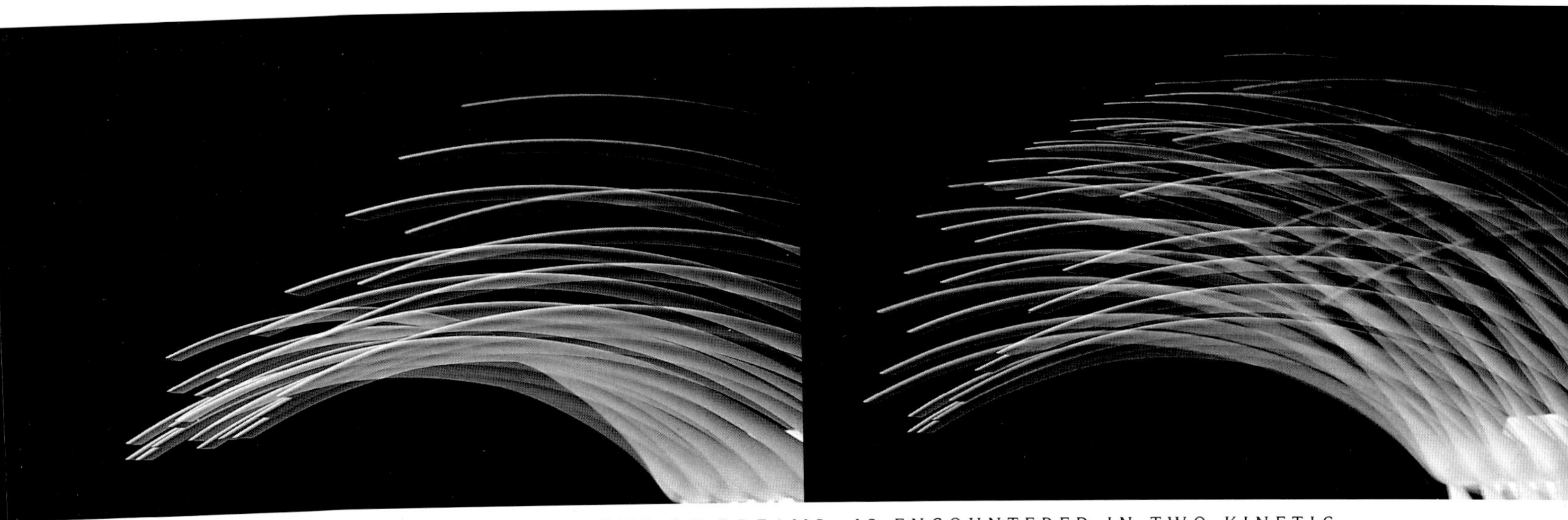

A TYPICAL THEME OF DREAMS, IS ENCOUNTERED IN TWO KINETIC, WING-LIKE STRUCTURES NO MATTER HOW OFTEN WE EXPERIENCE THEIR SLOW, PERPETUAL, HYPNOTIC MOVEMENT EMANATING FROM THE MORE SIMPLE MOVEMENT OF EACH INDIVIDUAL ELEMENT, THEY IMPART A STRANGE FEELING THAT, ... THEY ARE ALIVE.

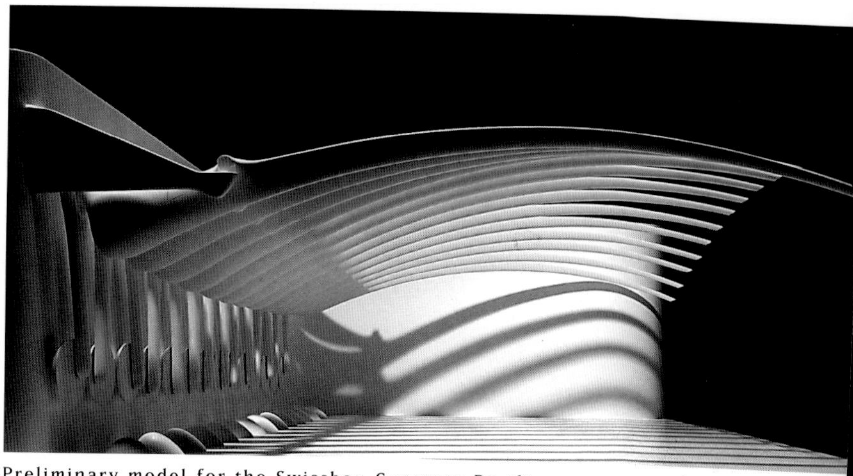

Preliminary model for the Swissbau Concrete Pavilion.

Dream-Work and Moving Structures

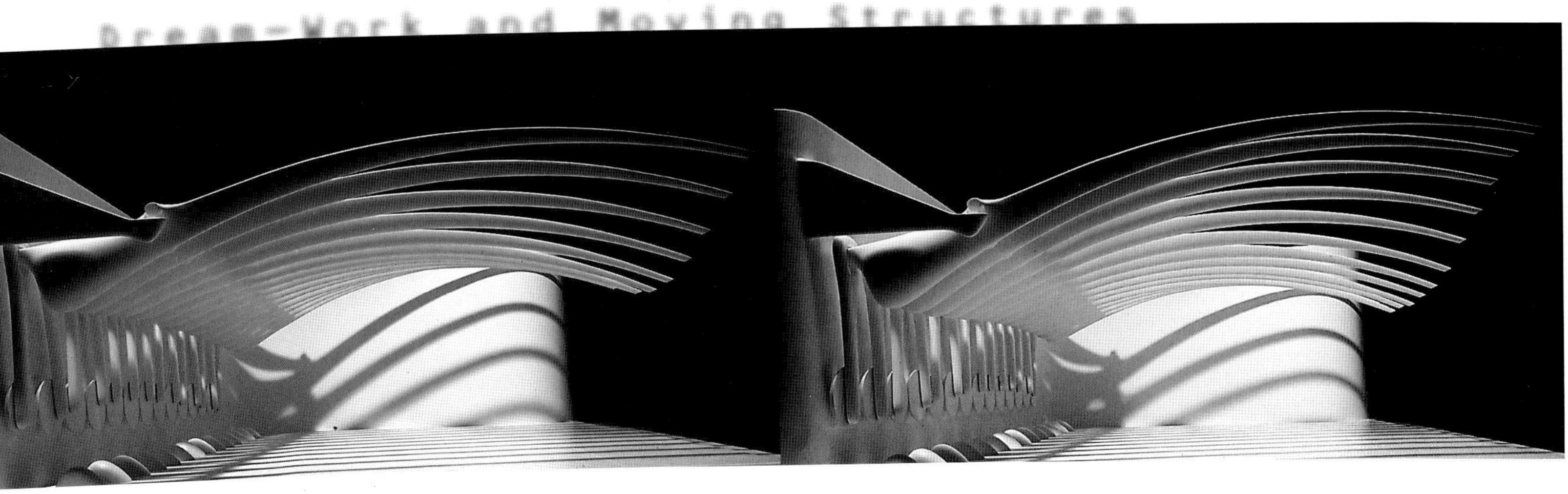

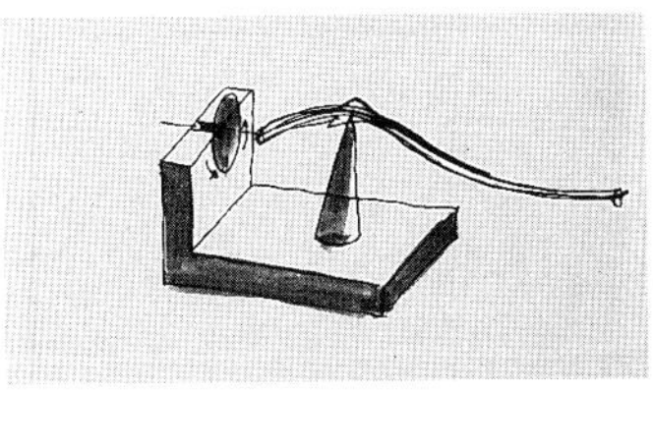

relatively light, demand modest energy to overcome the machine's inertia, and are easy to polish perfectly. Additionally, they are low friction materials which, having a good 'modulus of elasticity', for example — a very important quality since machine components often operate under significant stress — have the added benefit of structural soundness. By expecting concrete to perform in a manner normally associated with other materials, in other words by putting a new material to an old use, these moving sculptures created an opportunity to learn about materials, structure and movement. The viewer is encouraged to focus and reflect on both machine and material. This could have been achieved in a boring, didactic manner, but Calatrava's design stresses the use of concrete in a strange, out of the ordinary manner, to generate an oniric tension and excitement.

Floating Pavilion to commemorate the anniversary of the Swiss Confederation (project). Sketch 1989.

THERE are even more intriguing elements waiting to be discovered in these moving structures: in their imitation of nature, as revealed by the shape of the mobile members, there is an undeniable biomorphic analogy. To a certain degree, they remind us of attempts by most Picturesque, Art Nouveau or Organic designers at mimicking the products of nature, simulating their external form. But with their almost imperceptibly slow, restrained and rhythmical motions, and their shapes so difficult to unambiguously relate to a concrete object, Calatrava's structures create associations that are unusual amongst these designers, namely dream-work associations.

WITHIN Calatrava's oeuvre, the theme of

structures in flight and its accompanying dream-work have migrated from these sculptures to two most extraordinary and idiosyncratic architectural designs: the project for a floating pavilion on Lake Lucerne to celebrate the 700th anniversary of the Swiss Confederation, and the Kuwait Pavilion at the Expo 92, in Seville. Both were conceived in the tradition of the building type named "ephemera": temporary light-weight structures with a long tradition of fantastic and dream-like effects. Yet in both projects, the movement of the roof structures also fulfils functional needs: as in the Swiss Confederation building, the 25 metre high cantilevered members of the Kuwait Pavilion come down to protect the visitors from the sun, rising up at night to accommodate the different uses of the terrace.

IN both projects, movement permits the structure of the roof to open and close. In the transformation that permits the metamorphosis of the open crown shape into a closed dome, the relevance of the foldability studies in Calatrava's thesis is evident — both in the kinetic mechanism and in the geometry of the individual members of the roof structures. The importance of Calatrava's thesis is also evident in another moving structure, namely the fountain for the Central Square in Alcoi (1991-1995). The mechanism, resembling a sheet of water folding and unfolding over a circular pool, is more akin to the doors of the Ernsting warehouse than the domes of the pavilions.

WITH the floating Swiss Confederation Pavilion, movement was enhanced by supporting the kinetic roof on a raft, gliding like a swan over the lake's surface; the pavilion was mobile, and could be towed to various locations out on the lake, or moored to the shore. Another structure by Calatrava — a phalanx of water jets that were also conceived to glide across the surface of the water — was to have accompanied it.

CALATRAVA'S Swiss Confederation and Kuwait Pavilions appear as objects

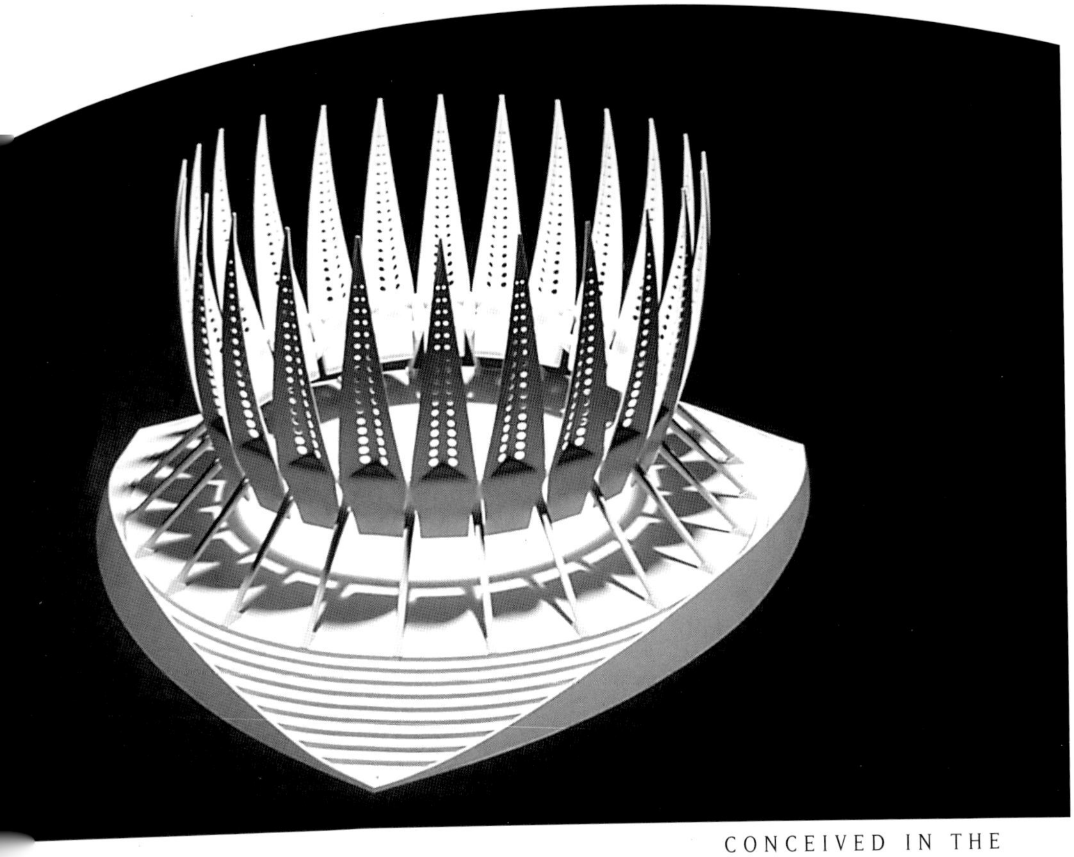

CONCEIVED IN THE TRADITION OF THE BUILDING TYPE NAMED "EPHEMERA": TEMPORARY LIGHT-WEIGHT STRUCTURES WITH A LONG TRADITION OF FANTASTIC AND DREAM-LIKE EFFECTS. YET IN BOTH PROJECTS, THE MOVEMENT OF THE ROOF STRUCTURES ALSO FULFILS FUNCTIONAL NEEDS:

Concrete Floating Pavilion

Kuwait Pavilion

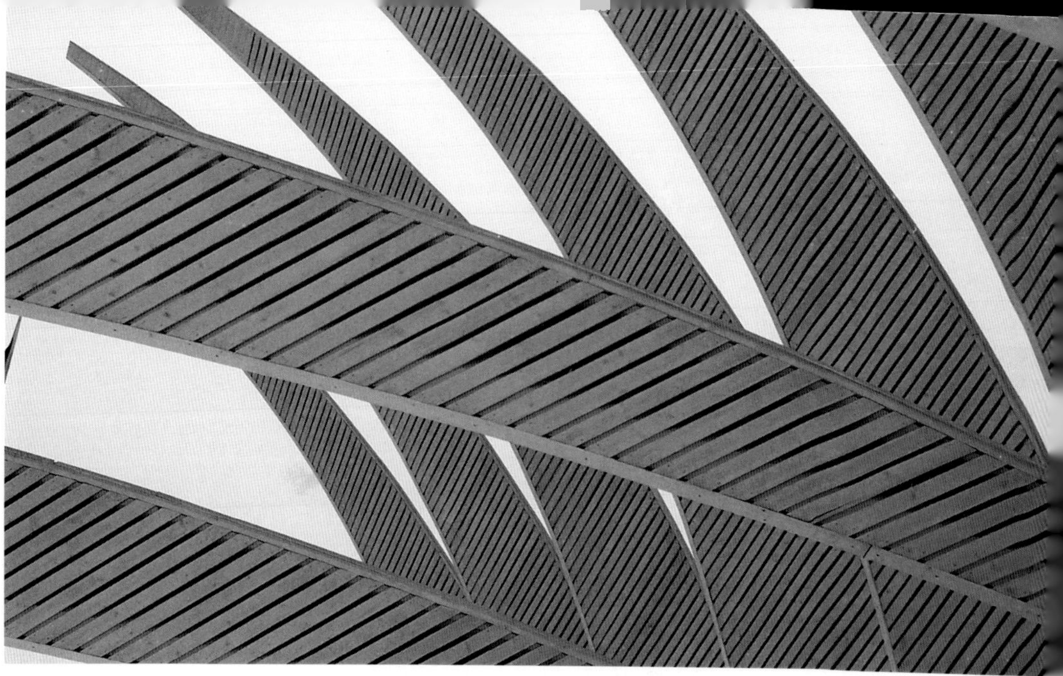

Kuwait Pavilion. The roof elements resemble waving palms.

Kuwait Pavilion

Dream-Work and Moving Structur

in a dream, not so much because of the presence of moving elements (moving roofs have been constructed since antiquity, a tradition that still marks many contemporary sports stadiums), but because their mobile elements convey the impression that the entire structure, although a building constructed of very heavy materials, is poised on the threshold of flight — like a swan, in the case of the Swiss Confederation Pavilion; like a falcon, with Kuwait's Pavilion.

BUT there is another dream-work aspect in the moving structures of these pavilions. Freud wrote in The Interpretation of Dreams: "The way in which dreams treat the category of contraries and contradictories is highly remarkable. It is simply disregarded. 'No' seems not to exist so far as dreams are concerned. They show a particular preference for combining contraries into a unity or for representing them as one and the same thing. Dreams feel themselves at liberty." As a result of this tendency to break down contraries and contradictories, the objects created through dream-work tend to be "composite structures" (p.383).

15. Siegfried Giedion, *Space, Time and Architecture*, Cambridge, 3rd expanded edition, 1959, p. 286.

THIS is exactly what occurs in the Swiss Confederation Pavilion: superimposed upon the image of a swan's wings is another image: the pavilion as a slowly dilating water lily. A third image, an opening and closing eye, is in turn superimposed on this water lily; all are integrated into a new cognitive composite. In the Kuwait Pavilion, there is similar agreement in the superimposition of meanings on the moving elements of the structure: spreading falcon wings become waving palms; clashing scimitars become lashes that close to protect the eye against the harshness of the sun.

THE image of the eye returns, this time in the mechanism of the mobile roof structure in Calatrava's planetarium, at the Science Centre in Valencia. The traditional function (scientific observation) of a planetarium's opening dome is once more given an oniric quality as it opens and closes like an immense eye attached to the body of the earth. Anthropomorphic and anatomical associations also arise out of the Communications Tower in Seville, as it opens and closes at its base.

SUPERIMPOSITION is again the theme of Calatrava's 1988 project for the Bauschänzli restaurant on a fortress island in the centre of Zurich. Related to a system of nine glass and metal structures, these structures move, to either cover the facility or reveal the sky, and thus achieve a microclimatic flexibility. In moving, they combine as condensed and displaced objects, and can once again be seen in many different ways — as trees, umbrellas or wings.

MOVING through water rather than air is the theme of the Medoc swing bridge. A bridge with a moving deck that opens to let large vessels pass, thus avoiding the construction of a high deck, is nothing exceptional. There are many bridges with moveable parts. Giedion, for example, shows Arnodin's 1905 Ferry Bridge[15], in the old port of Marseilles, with moving parts. The Calatrava bridge is breathtaking as an idea, as much for its place within the realm of poetic dream-work as its technological innovation. To experience how the segment of the structure breaks free when it begins to rotate, released for a moment from the static, orderly world to become part of the river's flow and swell, metamorphosed into a gliding windjammer, plying the current, is like watching a bridge fulfilling a wish.

Dream-Work and Moving Structures

Initial design for the entrance to the metro station in Valencia.

Fountain. Central Square in Alcoi, Spain. 1991-95.

Dream-Work and Moving Str

Model of the Planetarium Building. Science Centre, Valencia. In progress.

and Moving Structures

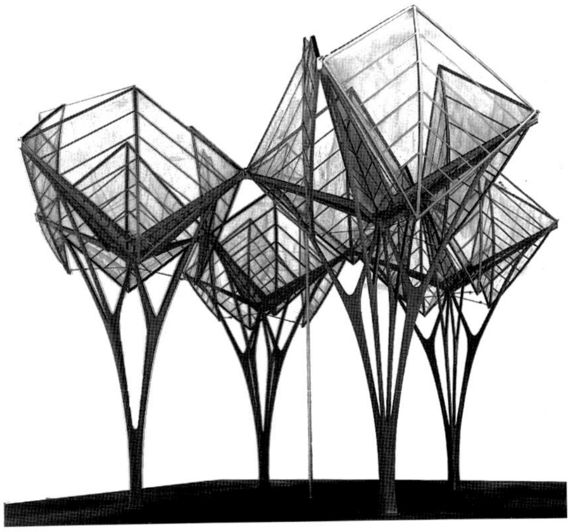

Model of the Bauschänzli Restaurant. Zurich (project).

Communication Tower. Barcelona

Base of the Communication Tower. Barcelona.

TO EXPERIENCE HOW THE SEGMENT OF THE STRUCTURE BREAKS FREE WHEN IT BEGINS TO ROTATE, RELEASED FOR A MOMENT FROM THE STATIC, ORDERLY WORLD TO BECOME PART OF THE RIVER'S FLOW AND SWELL, METAMORPHOSED INTO A GLIDING WINDJAMMER, PLYING THE CURRENT, IS LIKE WATCHING A BRIDGE FULFILLING A WISH.

Medoc Bridge

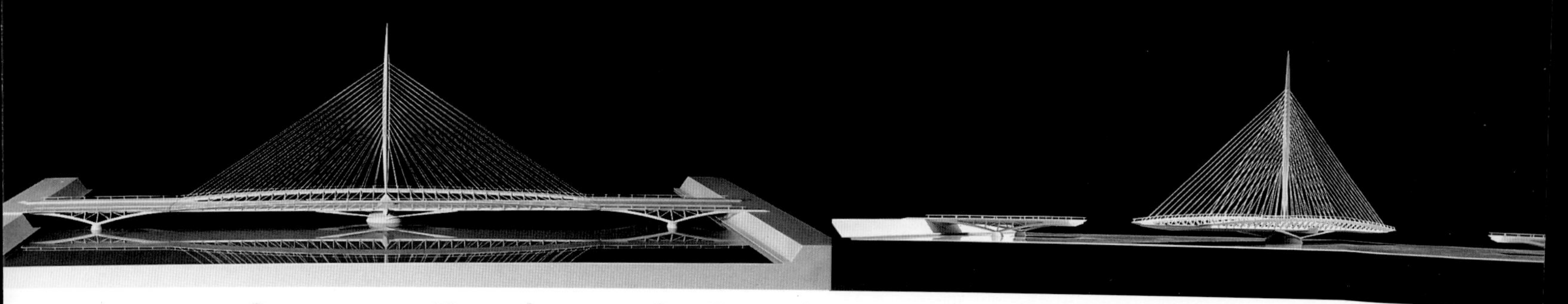

Model of the Medoc Swing Bridge (project). 1991.

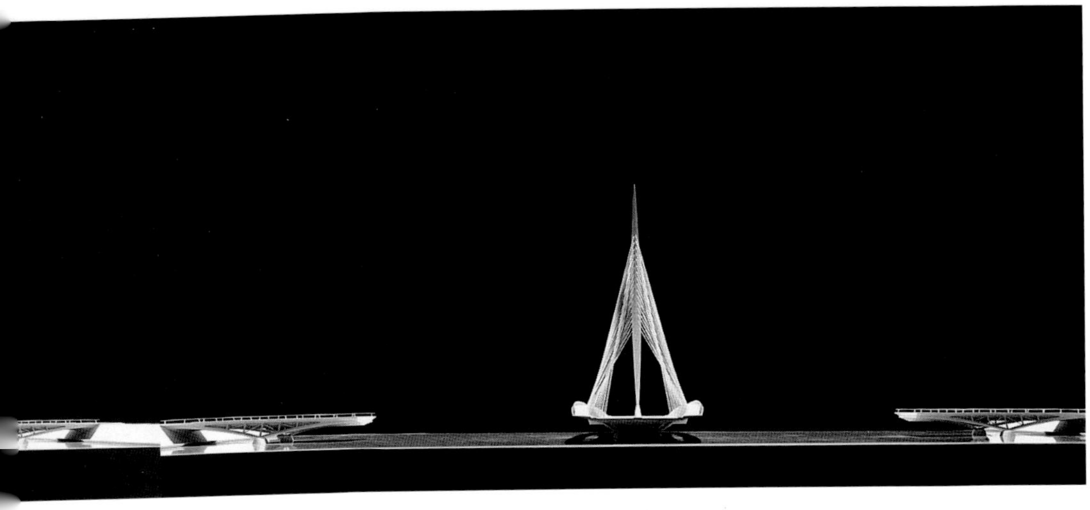

Reichstag Conversion Competition

Calatrava's Project for the Reichstag Conversion Competition. 1992.
Dome with the four movable roof segments.

SHEET OF CORRUGATED METAL, ABOUT ONE AND A HALF METRES BY FIVE, BALANCED ON ITS PYRAMID BASE AND RIPPLING...LIKE THE SURFACE OF WATER ON A CALM DAY;...THERE IS PERHAPS NOTHING "LATENT"...OTHER THAN AN EXPRESSION OF THE NEED OF THE HUMAN MIND TO DREAM.

Waves

Dream-Work and Mov

Calatrava's "Book in Flight". 1993.

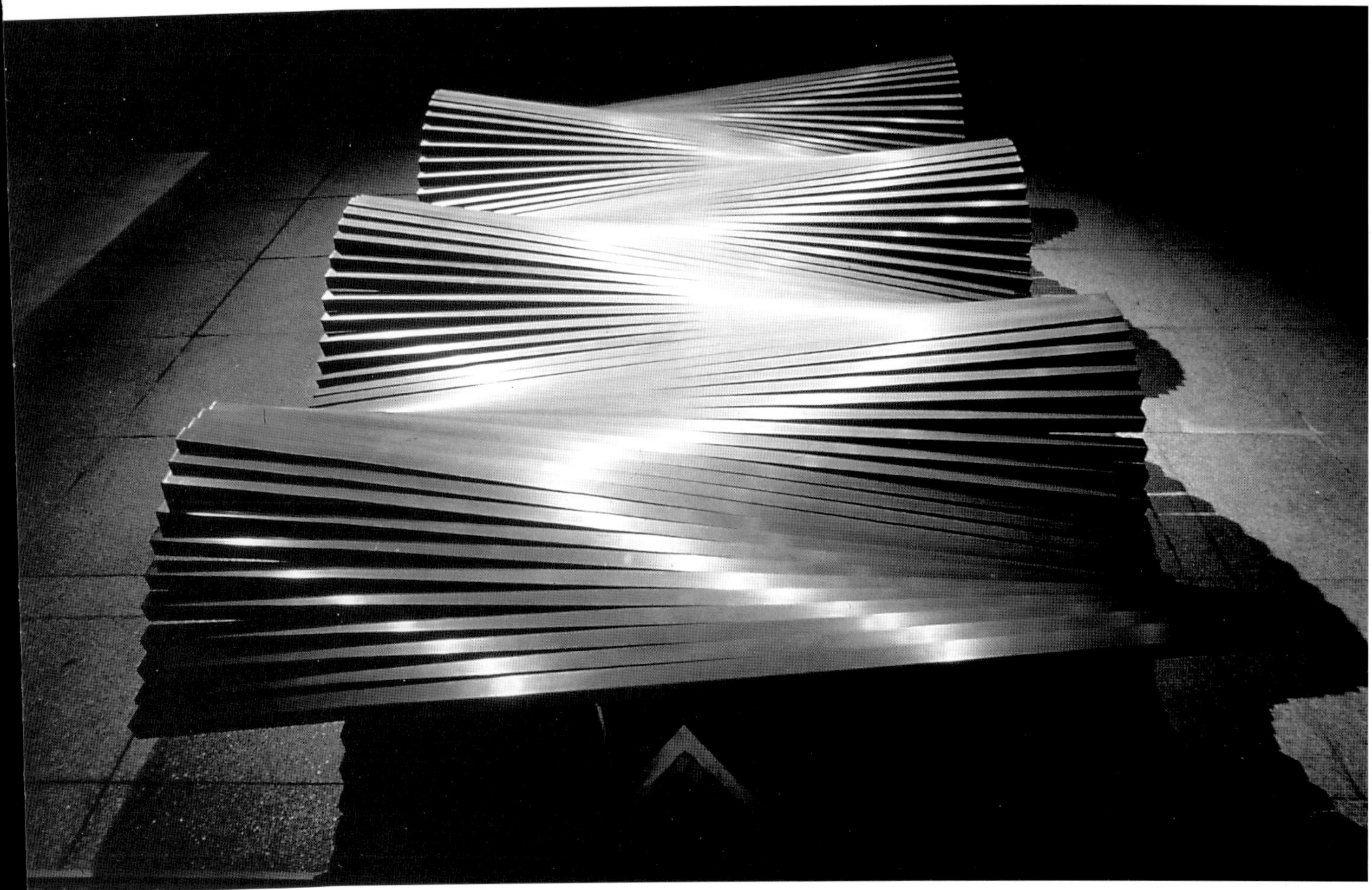

ON a very different scale (close to the sublime, one might almost say) is Calatrava's Reichstag conversion — a scheme for a new glass dome to replace the old dome, part of the original building designed by Paul Wallot between 1884-1894 that was destroyed in the 1933 fire. Here, the four roof segments open to the sky, creating in their movement the image of a gigantic flower that blooms above the massive building.

LIKE Etienne-Jules Marey and Frank Gilbreth, 19th century pioneers of the moving picture, Calatrava employs his structures as a means of "picturing time", to borrow a term from Marta Braun. But dreams are often at their most powerful when most directionless and divorced from pragmatics, and closest to poetry. This is born out in a very recent series of kinetic sculptures by Santiago Calatrava. One is composed of about a hundred 2mm thick, rigid, slender and gleaming metal pipes of about 8 metres height: arranged on a square base, these long and slender shafts eject a thin taper of water from their tips as they rotate slowly in unison to evoke stalks of wheat, swaying in the breeze; another is a sheet of corrugated metal, about one and a half metres by five, balanced on its pyramid base and rippling in an asymmetrical, hyperbolic and parabolic motion like the surface of water on a calm day; another is like the pages of an open book, with flat wooden slats that rise and fall like the wings of a bird. All are animated with the oniric, slow-motion rhythm common to all of Calatrava's moving structures. As in many dream-works, there is perhaps nothing "latent" in these works, other than an expression of the need of the human mind to dream.

Etienne-Jules Marey. Flight of a Seagull. 1886. Collège de France.

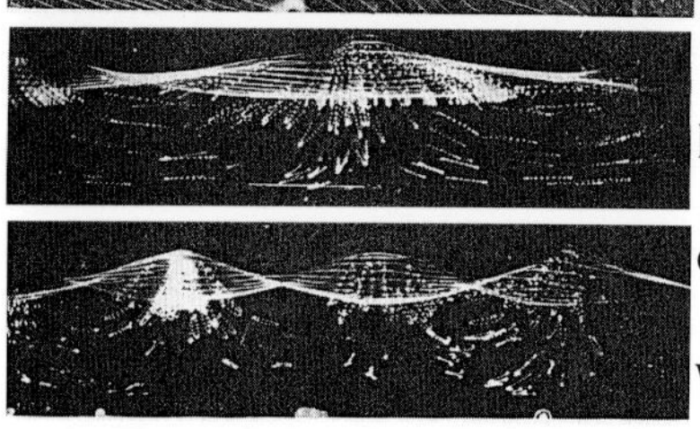

Etienne-Jules Marey. Studies of the movement of waves. 1893. Glass Slides. Collège de France.

Calatrava's kinetic fountain entitled "Stalks of Wheat". Project for the Fondation Cartier. 1994.

Modell "Cross of Waves"

Structure and Flow

THE actual motion of structural components and the creation of dream-work is one way in which structures can relate to movement. Another, functional way is the accommodation of the movement of people and things. Once more, the relationship between movement and structure not only becomes the subject for a problem-solving process, but also the point of departure for poetics.

SINCE 1945, there have been several fascinating examples of designs for railway stations and air terminals which have related structure and movement through the invention of novel spatial arrangements. The Stadelhofen railway station in Zurich stands apart as probably the most remarkable among these projects — an example of an architectural-infrastructure project that spatially relates structure and movement.

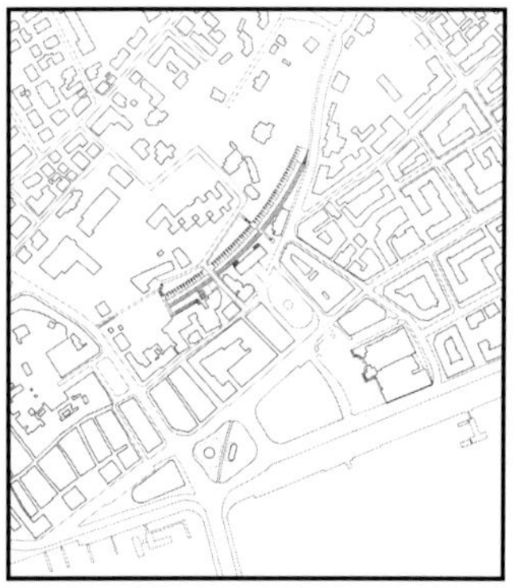

Stadelhofen Train Station. 1983-90. Site plan.

THIS project for the Swiss Federal Railways, intended to cope with a sharp and immediate increase in traffic, was awarded first prize in an open competition in 1982. The highly constrained site, once the fortified edge of the city and restricted by the hill contour, the alluvial plain, the existing urban fabric and the extreme differences in level, appears to have stimulated rather than suppressed the uniqueness, and ultimately the inventiveness, of the design.

THE 270 metre complex excels in its integration of public transportation, urban context and natural setting into a single complementary, rather than conflicting, whole. Its unique success lies in the conception of Stadelhofen not so much as a composition of volumes, but as an organisation of coexisting, cooperating sub-systems accommodating the complicated flow of urban life.

THE way in which each circulation mode in the scheme has been allocated an individual realm of conduits is the main characteristic of the Stadelhofen form as an organisation of sub-systems. The result is a three dimensional, well-woven network of different scales and movement qualities. The way in which distinctive points of transition, interchange and exchange relate each movement sub-system to other movements within this network further contributes to a conception of the scheme as a three dimensional network, referred to by Calatrava as "design by section".

IN his adherence to "the section" as a design tool — once again a result of his invaluable background in engineering — Calatrava is almost alone in his profession. As has been shown by all major precedents of equivalent urban complexes, according to the operational requirements of each of the specific circulation sub-systems and, ultimately, its spatial quality, a designer can envisage a building's micro-zoning layout by means of the conventions represented in the section of a building complex. As Calatrava once stated: "the section is not only linked to the strength of the building, to the way in which forces flow through it, but also to its beauty".

THIS should certainly not imply that representation dictates the form of a scheme and, even worse, that drawing is a goal in itself. As Calatrava also observed: "Drawing and architecture are two different things. Architecture...emanates more from the world of ideas directly applied to the materials used in a building. Graphics intervene". In a more polemical mood he added: "They have almost become a hindrance." The point is that, rather than being a purely visual process, in the last analysis design is a complex, cognitive process involving spatial as well as time and action schemata. History has shown that a graphic means of representation can help and even revolutionise thinking about complex spatial objects and processes, as long as these graphic descriptions can, through visual means, map aspects of movement and function.

THE analysis of a complex multilayer and multisystem organisation is also a result of Calatrava's fascination with anatomical section drawings. For the guidance of surgeons, Leonardo da Vinci believed that the anatomical section drawing was superior in many respects to the spectacle of "an anatomist to work"[16], and since its invention in the Renaissance he has been proven correct. As also demonstrated by Leonardo, the development of the section drawing for guiding designers was equally significant, especially in the conception of building projects with a complex infrastructure, accommodating multiple flows and involving the differentiation and articulation of several functional transportation components and their multilevel spatial composition.

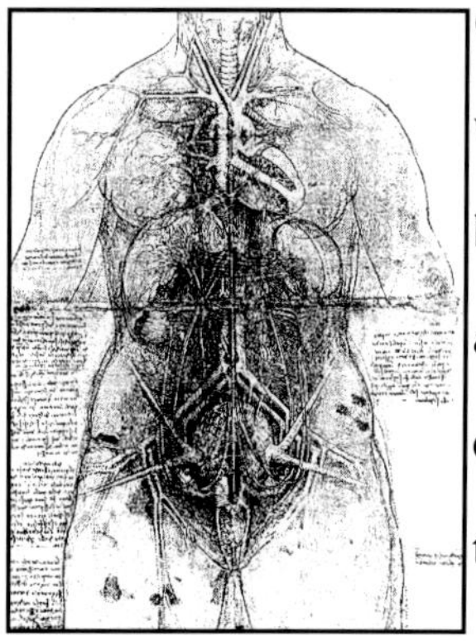

Leonardo da Vinci. "Situs Figure". (W 12281 r; K/P 122 r).

WITH its manifold richness of diverse and specialised layers, spatially coordinated and controlled in a most compacted way, the plan of Stadelhofen as a host of multiple flows resembles an organism. Rather than frustrating the designer, the constraints of the site, the landscape contour and the existing buildings have combined to assist the development of a highly inventive, efficient solution. These factors have stimulated the conception of a well-packed arrangement of tightly interlocked, superposed and specialised components. In its effective compactness, this arrangement resembles the joining of anatomical organs, and has also dictated the graceful curve of the train tracks with its 400 metre radius, further enhancing the 'organic' appearance of the scheme.

WITHIN the body of the station, paths, passes and passages are interlinked into a well-tempered, well-formed, harmoniously orchestrated universe accommodating different flow types: the fast regular flow of trains along the tracks cutting through the ground level; the hasty pedestrian flow entering and leaving the vehicles along the platforms, approaching and leaving the station, ascending and descending its three levels, mingling or walking through the shopping centre, which extends under the tracks to additionally serve as an underpass; the flow of pedestrians crossing above the tracks

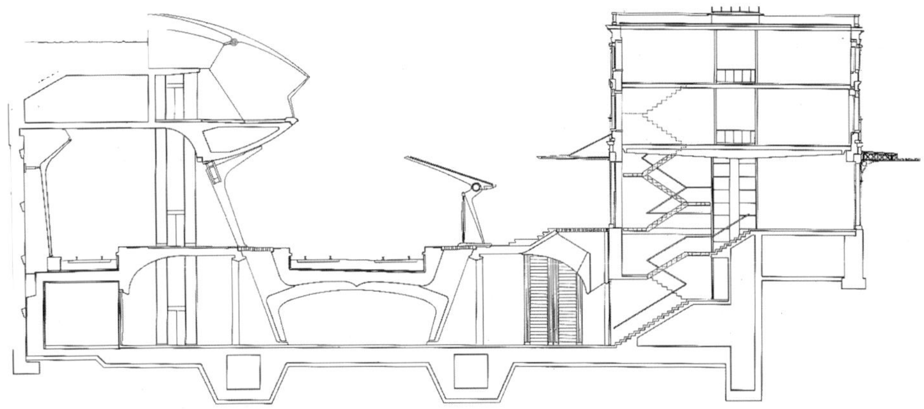

Stadelhofen Train Station. 1983-90. Section.

3
A

Stadelhofen Train Station

Structure and Flow

WITHIN THE BODY OF THE STATION, PATHS, PASSES
AND PASSAGES ARE INTERLINKED INTO A WELL-TEMPERED,
WELL-FORMED, HARMONIOUSLY ORCHESTRATED UNIVERSE
ACCOMMODATING DIFFERENT FLOW TYPES:
... FLOW OF TRAINS ...
PEDESTRIAN FLOW ENTERING ...
LEAVING ...,
APPROACHING ...
ASCENDING ...
DESCENDING ...
CROSSING ...
TRANSVERSING ...
STROLLING

Stadelhofen Train Station

over three steel bridges, transversing both hillside and plain to access the existing road system; the slow, leisurely flow of baudelairian "flaneurs", couples and small groups, strolling down the hill, along the promenade, down through the stairs and escalators to the shopping area and out onto the street.

THERE is, too, a flow that is indirectly seen, namely the flow of forces channeled down to the ground via the intricate configurations of the structure: the various materials such as steel, ferrovitreous and reinforced concrete, and elements such as columns, beams, cantilevers, platforms and supporting walls. We have already touched upon the way that the form of these structural components explicitly relates to movement, and how, by giving a specific geometrical shape to the various parts of the structure, these elements can resist external forces more efficiently and effectively. We can see, for example, how the columns of Stadelhofen branch into a Y-configuration, and so enhance their structural performance.

FINALLY, there are two further flow types which also contribute to the design of the station as a synthesis of movements: firstly, the penetrating flow of light filtering down to the shopping centre through the cantilevered glass and metal roof and the glass blocks of the sidewalks on the platform level, and secondly, a genuinely 'organic' flow of 'protoplasm' running through the branches and stems of the vines spreading over the cables of the steel pergola that sweeps back from the promenade's edge towards the hill.

IN most of Calatrava's works we see the same conceptional principles that regard structure as a three dimensional well-woven network containing differentiated conduits dedicated to different scales and qualities of movement. In the Lusitania motor and pedestrian bridge for Merida, commissioned by the Council of Extremadura in Spain, the pedestrian channel varies in level and, in an almost critical reversal of common practice, is accommodated in the structure in a predominant position, both above and separating the vehicle deck. A similar practice, separating the pedestrian and vehicular flows and allocating the higher level to pedestrians, is followed with the cable-stayed, 240 metre Medoc swing bridge, with its central base. In this case, the pedestrian decks are placed at the outer sides of the bridge. An invited entry for a competition organised by the Direction des Services Techniques of the city of Bordeaux, the section of the bridge provided sufficient space on the lower vehicle conduit for views out over the water — a visual flow channel, so to speak, for the motorists.

ESPECIALLY intriguing in the work of Calatrava is the coincidence and cooperation between two or more conduits within the same structure. The stepped entrance to the footpath of the Bach de Roda-Felipe II bridge, in Barcelona, is an example: the ascending stair and ascending arch join to form a multifunctional container within which the integrity of each flow is equally preserved. Further on, the flow of pedestrian movement intercepts the flow of forces, cutting through the middle of the concrete arch support at exactly the point where the resulting void does not weaken the structure; in other words, where the presence of material is redundant. In the same project, the channel for lighting is embedded in the channel for the handrail, and follows

Structure and Flow

STRUCTURE AS A THREE DIMENSIONAL
WELL-WOVEN NETWORK CONTAINING DIFFERENTIATED CONDUITS
DEDICATED TO DIFFERENT SCALES AND
QUALITIES OF MOVEMENT...
THE PEDESTRIAN CHANNEL ...
ACCOMMODATED IN ...
A PREDOMINANT POSITION, BOTH ABOVE AND
SEPARATING THE VEHICLE DECK...
THE HIGHER LEVEL TO PEDESTRIANS

Lusitania Bridge

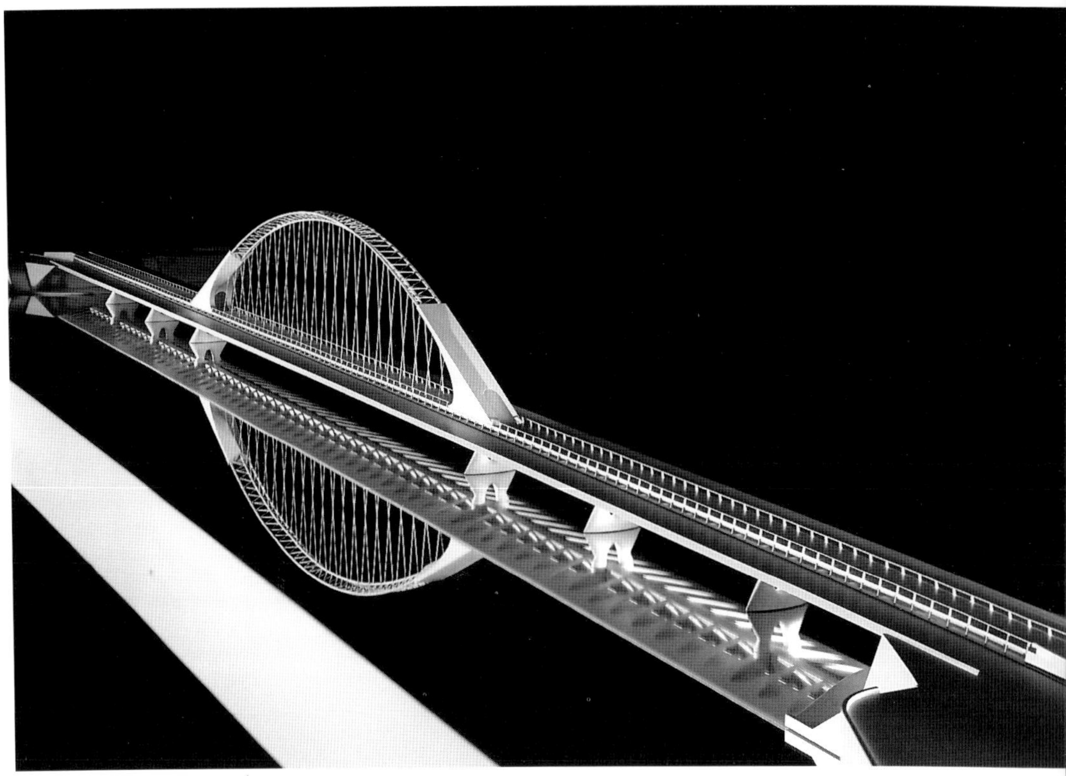

Bach de Roda Bridge

ESPECIALLY INTRIGUING...IS THE COINCIDENCE AND COOPERATION BETWEEN TWO OR MORE CONDUITS WITHIN THE SAME STRUCTURE. ...THE ASCENDING STAIR AND ASCENDING ARCH JOIN TO FORM A MULTIFUNCTIONAL CONTAINER WITHIN WHICH THE INTEGRITY OF EACH FLOW IS EQUALLY PRESERVED

... THE CONFIGURATION OF THE ROOF ... SATISFIES THE REQUIREMENT FOR TRAVELLER ORIENTATION ... GIVING THE COMPLEX ITS UNIQUE, HIGHLY RECOGNISABLE, IDENTIFIABLE AND MEMORABLE IMAGE OF MOVEMENT.

Satolas TGV Station

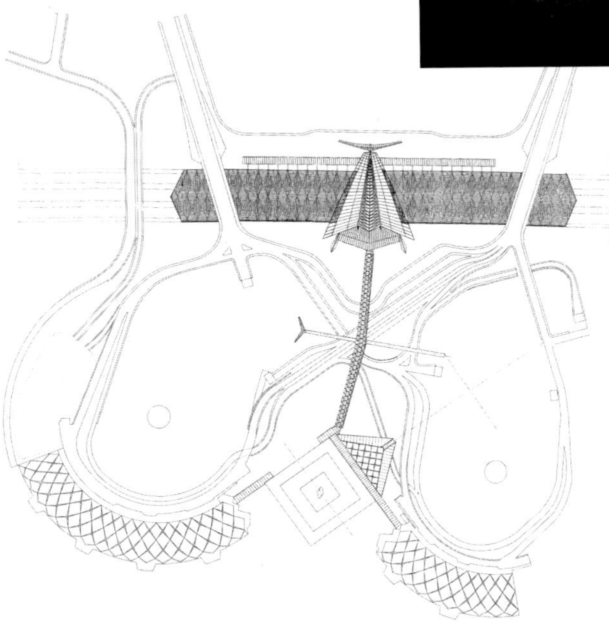

Satolas TGV Station Structure and Flow

the same rules of differentiation between flows, articulation of channels and spatial cooperation between channels.

CALATRAVA'S railway station at Lyon-Satolas for the TGV high speed trains is also the result of a competition. The station is an outstanding example of an elaborate structure, conceived as a mega-vessel to accommodate a highly demanding complex of movements. Contrary to the Stadelhofen station, with its tight site conditions within the existing historical city fabric and hill topography, the site of the Lyon-Satolas station did not impose immediate constraints on the form of the structure. Although the program was demanding, it was less heterogeneous. Basically, the scheme comprises a main station building, with train platforms and a passageway connecting the station to the adjacent airport which it serves. In dictating the kinds of movement and the flow of trains, buses, cars and pedestrians that the building was to accommodate, the functional requirements of the program demanded great attention to design detail but, as opposed to Stadelhofen, did not require a highly differentiated and compact solution. For the Satolas program, however, there was a special stipulation related to movement: good passenger orientation. This explains the size and directionality of the volumes of the complex, and justifies the emphasis on the rhythmical pattern of the repetitive members of the structure, appearing like a parade alongside the more major movement of the crowds. The need for orientation also explains the modulation of light, also defined in a directional and rhythmical way, which is more sparse in the core of the station, becoming more penetrating with the movement of passengers towards the tracks, and the outside.

IT is, however, the configuration of the roof which probably satisfies the requirement for traveller orientation more than anything else, giving the complex its unique, highly recognisable, identifiable and memorable image of movement. This image is achieved through mimesis: shaping of the roof to resemble the silhouette of a gigantic bird "that unfolds its wings longitudinally over the platforms" as if ready to land, or take off and soar.

Structures, Icons of Movement

STRUCTURES that move and which, in so doing, resemble organisms that move, are offset by a long tradition of designing structures that, even when static, resemble objects in motion.

THERE are the simulacra of the slow movement of growing plants or trees attached to the structural members of buildings: the palm-leaf or scallops of the Philae capitals of Egypt; the acanthus on the Corinthian capitals of Greek and Roman antiquity; the foliated or flowing arches, tracery, vaulted roofs of Gothic construction; the imitations of botanical forms by Baroque architects such as Jose or Juaquin de Churiguera; the vegetal originals of more recent architects such as Louis Sullivan or Hector Guimard. In the work of Victor Horta, vegetal forms will occasionally even influence the basic characteristics of the structure's configuration.

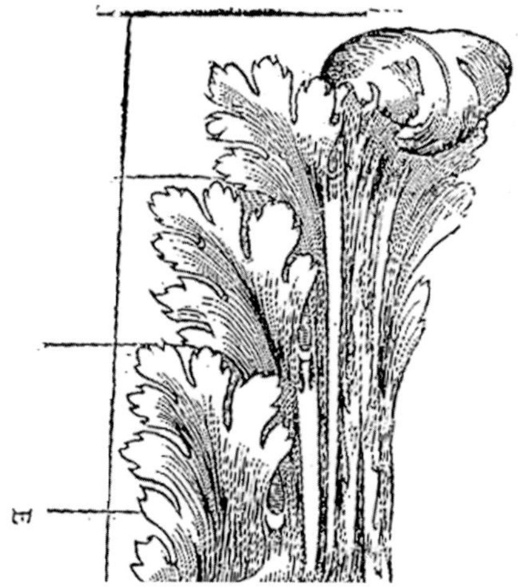

Acanthus, from Philibert de l'Orme, De l'architecture, Rouen, 1648. Livre V, p. 149.

IN addition to Lyon-Satolas, there are other projects by Calatrava where movement appears linked to structure through imitation. Without doubt, the roof of the projected new Airport Terminal for Sondica in Bilbao, Spain, gives the impression of a great bird with open wings. So, too, does the 1990 Auditorium and Conference Hall for Santa Cruz, Tenerife, in the Canary Islands. The scheme for two auditoria — a main hall for 2000 people and a smaller space for 400 — with the spectacular curving prow of the main roof, in fact resembles a 1986 sculpture explicitly entitled "The Bird". Bringing movement into structure through the pictorial representation of a bird is not confined only to projects dedicated to movement, such as transportation terminals. The bird theme emerges in the schemes of many other Calatrava projects, regardless of their actual function.

ALONG with these projects and the mobile structures so far mentioned, in aggrandising the image of a bird to huge proportions, the Lyon-Satolas station creates an oniric aura of the idea of flying that goes beyond the illusory effect of realistic mimesis. Beyond any superficial likeness of the design to a specific organism which flies (such as a bird), we can discover more abstract qualities in the form of a structure that represents movement. Such a representation relates structure and movement generatively, in the manner in which a structure embodies the movement involved in its genesis.

Bilbao Airport

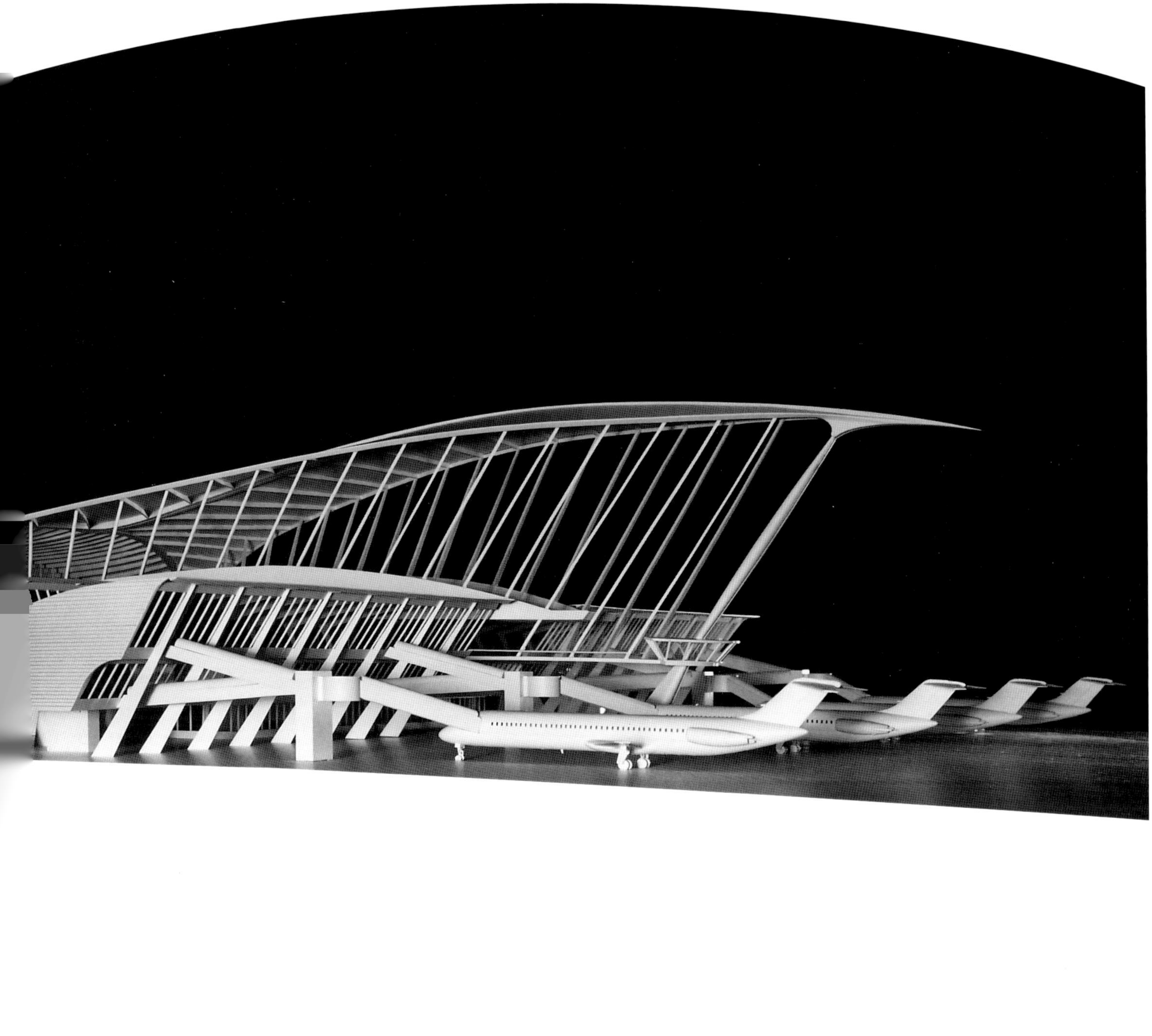

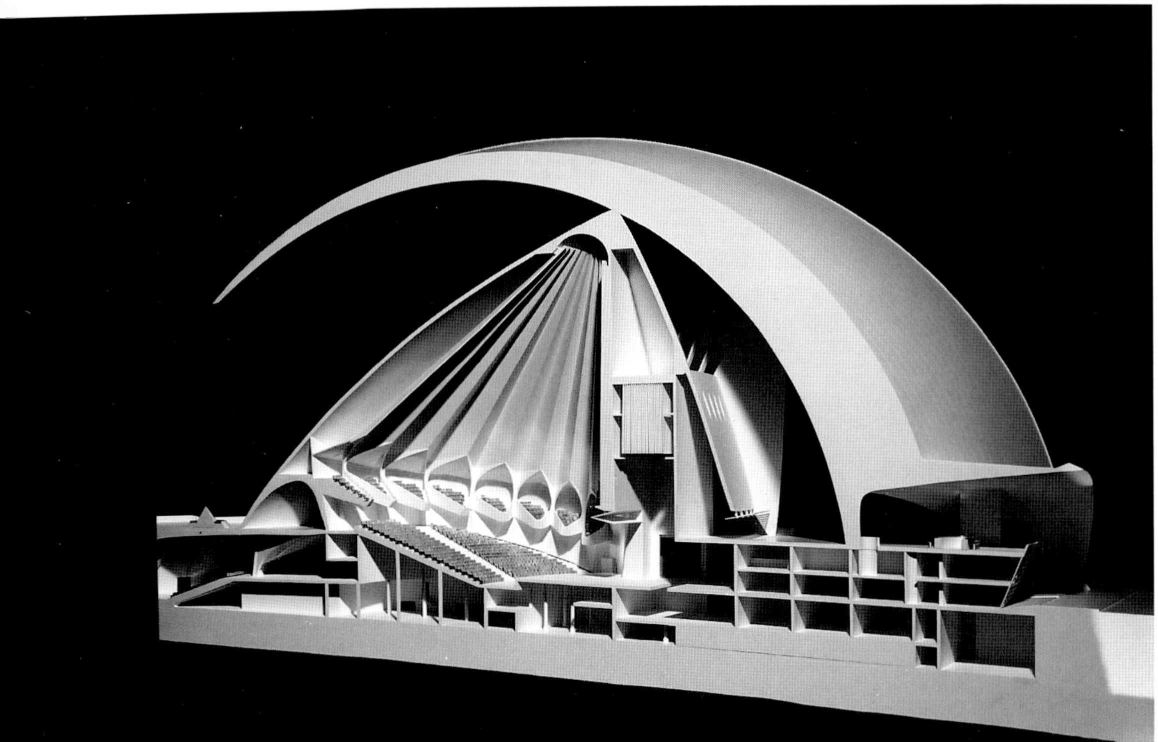

The Pecking Bird

Satolas TGV Station

Structures, Icons of

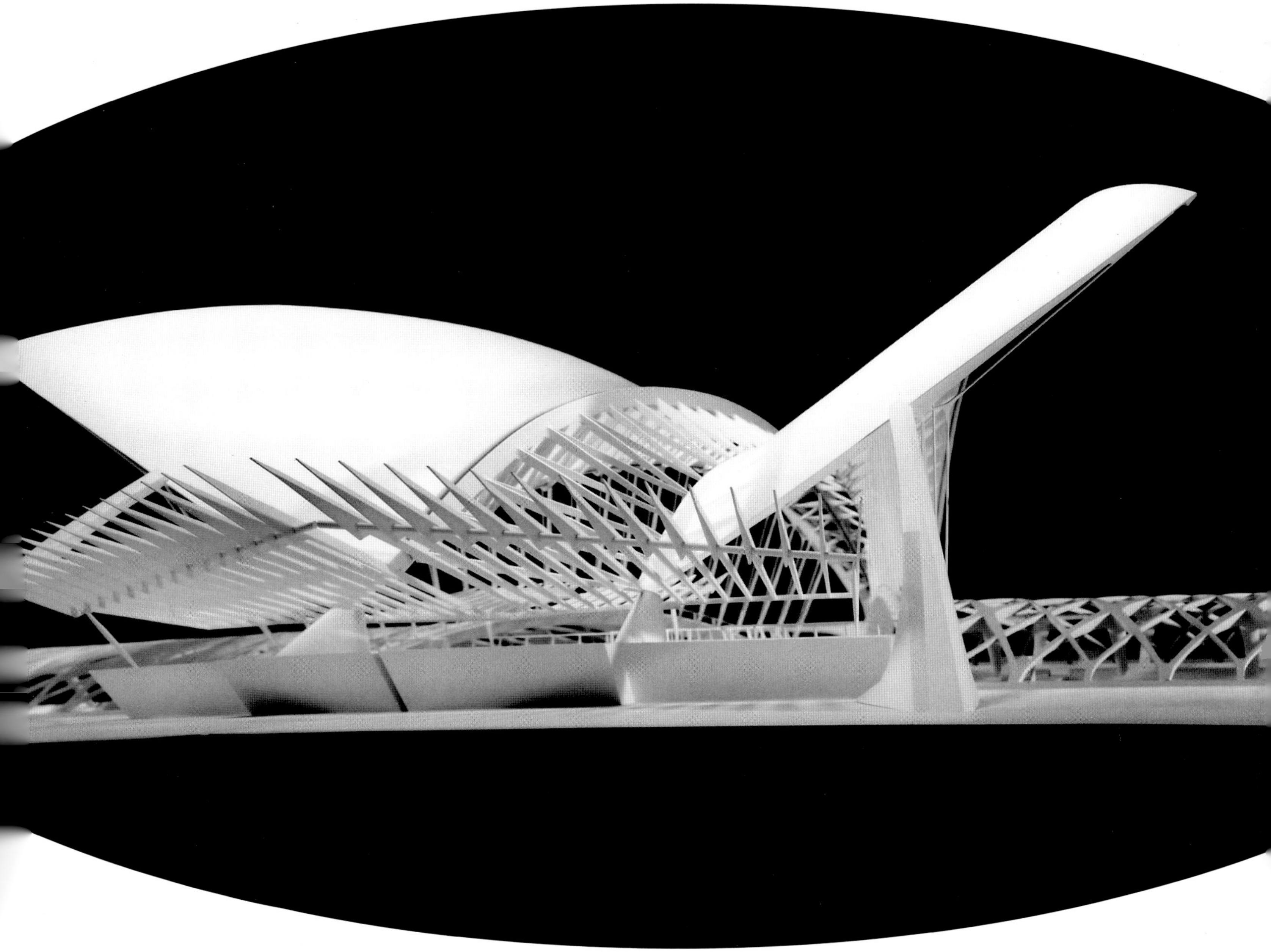

Movements Memory and Constructional Traces

WHETHER natural or artificial, structures are the result of movement. They are the products of the transportation of materials, and the components of assembly and construction. Indeed, even with regard to those structures which appear to negate the very idea of movement, without it they would not exist.

THE creation of structures involves movement of all kinds: transport; carrying; raising; grouping; rotating; dissolving; pouring; welding; bonding; nailing; joining; fastening; inflating. The list could include other kinds of movement: the movement of data, cash and ideas — all of which, most of the time, are part of the formation of a structure.

AS a general rule, behind the static reality of a structure can be found a complex, costly and occasionally risky record of people, material, information and machines in movement. Contrary to the movement of the glaciers of the Alps, whose paths are detectable directly from the geometry of the mountain structure, there is no such register for the movements responsible for most artificial structures. In fact, as Paul Valéry observed when discussing the work of Degas, "achieving" a project — bringing a work to its successful completion — is very often taken to imply the destruction of everything involved in its fabrication[17]. But as Valéry further remarked: "the work does not have to erase the traces of the work".

IF generative movements are to be committed to

17. Paul Valéry, *Degas, Danse, Dessin,* Paris 1938.

memory, and if such histories are to be chronicled, how can this be done? Can physical structures, through their form and dimensions, internally record their own complex history of emergence in any better way than an external archive of preliminary sketches which document the evolution of the evolution of the structure's form?

Construction process from Calatrava projects

Movements Memory and Constructional Traces

THE CREATION OF STRUCTURES INVOLVES MOVEMENT OF ALL KINDS: TRANSPORT; CARRYING; RAISING; GROUPING; ROTATING; DISSOLVING; POURING; WELDING; BONDING; NAILING; JOINING; FASTENING; INFLATING. THE LIST COULD INCLUDE OTHER KINDS OF MOVEMENT: THE MOVEMENT OF DATA, CASH AND IDEAS — ALL OF WHICH, MOST OF THE TIME, ARE PART OF THE FORMATION OF A STRUCTURE

Construction process and details.

Movements Memory and Constructional Traces

Movement Streamlining Structures

THE generative process giving rise to the structure of mountains has always aroused both awe and curiosity. From the dawning of civilisation, all over the world cosmological myths have attempted to explain the mountain's form through violent struggles in the past, whereby its structure incorporated into its shape the memory of primordial forces — awesome gods, events, unions, separations, strife.

IN the eighteenth century, the fascination with the structure of mountains, along with the "knowledge" of their "nature and structure"— to quote the Swiss pioneer of geology Horace Benedict de Saussure — took a scientific turn: in the context of a general "theory of the earth", Saussure believed that Mont-Blanc's unique shape contained "the key to a great system". Between 1764 and 1787, he undertook a number of expeditions — rather hard during those days — to "find a solution to the great problem of (its)...formation". He came to the conclusion that the solution was to be found in the nature of the movement of the glaciers: "chassent devant eux les terres et les pierres accumulées devant leurs glaces"[18]. According to Saussure, the configuration of the structure thus embodied the story of the movement that generated it.

OTHER studies followed Saussure's pioneering work, and explained the morphology of Alpine structures through the action of glaciers, torrents, or other kinds of movement. John Ruskin, in particular, dedicated a great

18. Horace Benedict de Saussure, *Voyage dans les Alpes*, Neuchâtel, 1786-97.

19. John Ruskin, *Modern Painters*, (4 vols.), Oxford, 1843 - 1860. The present discussion pertains to volume 4.

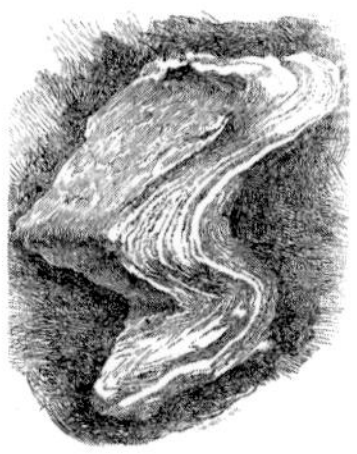

Illustrations of the Alps from John Ruskin, Modern Painters, Oxford, 1843-1860.

part of his studies to this topic. His best writings on the topic are contained in the fourth volume of the "Modern Painters", entitled Of Mountain Beauty, and particularly in chapters XII, XIII: On the Sculpture of Mountains and chapters XIV-XVII: Resulting Forms [19].

ALTHOUGH ostensibly about painting — and in particular the painting of Turner — Ruskin's study went beyond the optical aspects and the appearance of "masses and rocks" of mountains to explore the process that formed them. It searched for an explanation, and attempted to identify the "subtle complexity" and the "authoritative principle" underlying the form of the structure of the "mountain mass ... the inner anatomy which regulates growth and form". Ruskin's detailed arguments about the genesis of the structure of the Alps were based on empirical observations gathered in the field. They were expressed in magnificent prose and superb drawings, through which he tried to answer the "two questions" which for him were of the deepest interest: "From what first created forms were the mountains brought into their present condition? Into what forms will they change in the course of ages?"

RUSKIN opens his discussion about the "sculpture" of the mountain peak known as the Aiguille Charmoz. This peak, he maintains, was shaped by a "small stream descending from the foot of the granite peak." He describes his painstaking measurements, taken with the aid of a bottle of ordinary wine, in order to calculate the mass of earth being moved down through the "one of the weakest streams in the valley." He deduces that this "insignificant runlet...some four inches wide and four inches deep" was capable of displacing "more than two tons of the substance of Mont Blanc". Ruskin followed his measurements with a rough calculation of the overall movement of the gigantic mass throughout the entire mountain, and the changing form of its structure.

HILL profiles (divided by Ruskin into four "systems": Lines of Fall; Lines of

Projection; Lines of Escape; Lines of Rest), along with contours, contortions, regularities of position, summit peaks, recesses, aiguilles, crests, precipices, banks, right down to the "outline of (single) stones" — all those features that make up the identity of the complex structure of "these mysterious Alps" — are "results produced by action(s)" and by "power and motion". They are "torrent sculptures", "the deathfull crumbling of atom from atom in...corrupting stones", either "gradually effacing", "dissolving", "decomposing" or "hewed by the axe of God in a most violent way".

FOR Ruskin, the study of the Alps was intended to provide answers to questions about the general phenomena of a slow "destruction and renovation", affecting not only the structure of mountains but also the "dwelling-place of men". Ruskin attempted to juxtapose the mountain's original form — its "first rising and first sculpture" — with the current shape of mountain masses. From "the actual form of any mountain peak," he tried to "trace ... the shadow or skeleton of its former self". In order to identify the agent carrying out the colossal morphogenetic process shaping the structure of the Alps, he used the case of the "insignificant runlet" at the foot of the Aiguille Charmoz peak as an initial, tangible paradigm. In turn, he projected the Alps as the paradigm of an even more universal phenomenon, namely the emergence of structure out of process, out of movement.

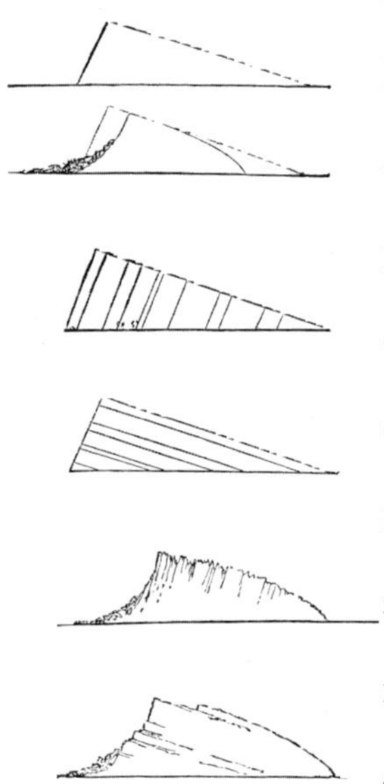

IN the final analysis, despite the realistic, rational and systematic character of his drawings and prose, and notwithstanding that certain observations (such as those about glaciers and erosion) are indeed of scientific value,

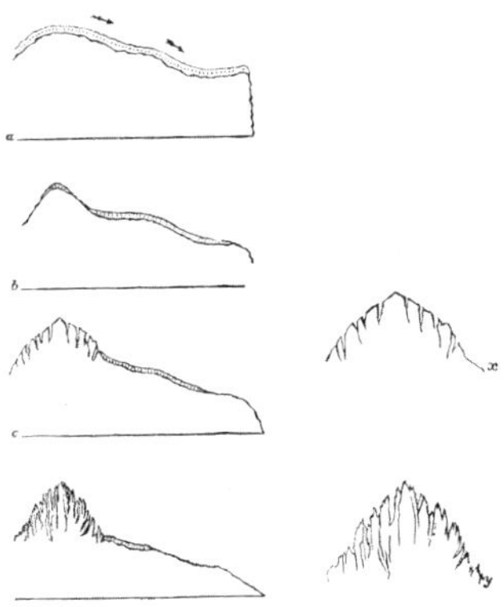

Illustrations of the Alps from John Ruskin, Modern Painters, Oxford, 1843-1860.

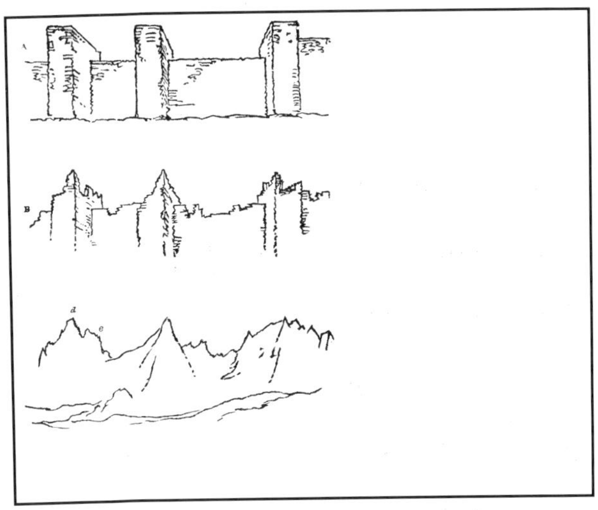

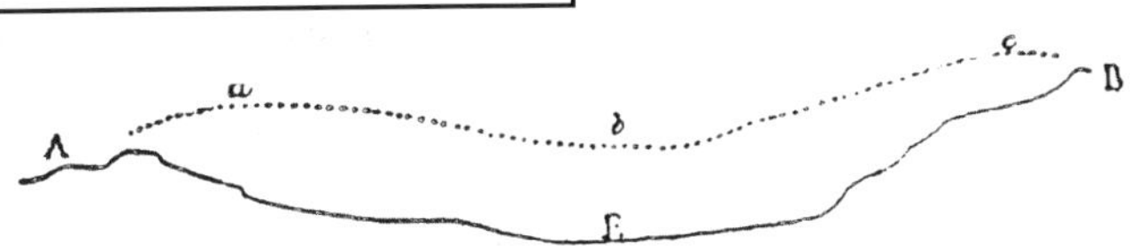

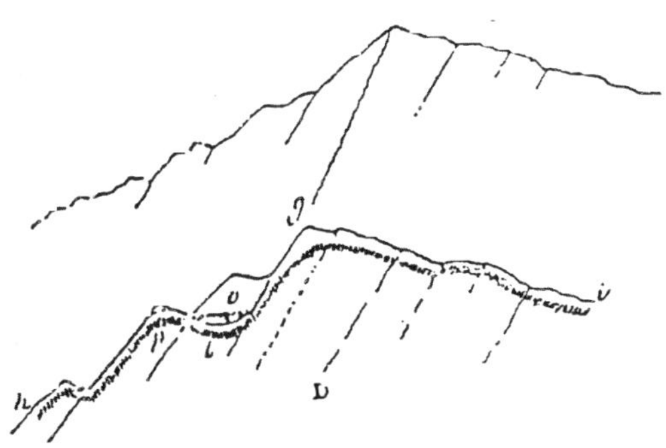

Ruskin's topography and morphology of the Alps is not that of a geologist. His is a "sentimental" — cognitive as we would say today — topology and topography. Beyond the moral, even political questions that Ruskin raises through the analogy of the historical processes of the destruction and renovation of natural forms, the significance of the Alps lies in their capacity to emotionally touch the onlooker through the "accumulation of memories" of movement which they represent.

A FEW years later, the fundamental processes behind the configuration of the Alps once again became the subject of intensive empirical studies, this time by the French architect Viollet-Le-Duc[20]. His diagrams and illustrations on the subject are even more numerous than Ruskin's. Rather than patchy examples, they are a complete documentation of the region. Although "sentimental" aspects appear to play no role in Viollet-Le-Duc's thinking, the main approach is the same as Ruskin's: to explain the current form of the structure of the mountain as a work of movement. In his 1874 Annuaire du Club Alpin Français, he expounds his thoughts in a brief text, accompanied by a series of diagrams which demonstrate how the present form of the mountain was produced by the processes of erosion and the movement of masses across lines of least resistance, in accordance with the laws of physics. He concludes: "Il n'y a rien là que de très naturel".

COMPLETE results of his empirical study were published two years later in his major work "Massif du

20. Eugene Viollet-le-Duc, *Massif du Mont Blanc. Etude sur la constitution géodesique, sur les transformations et sur l'état ancien et moderne de ses glaciers*. Paris 1876.

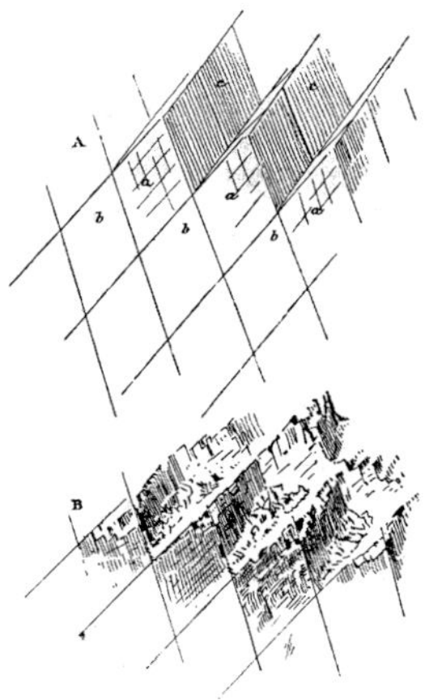

Massif of the Mont-Blanc.
From Viollet-le-Duc, Histoire du Mont-Blanc, Paris, 1876.

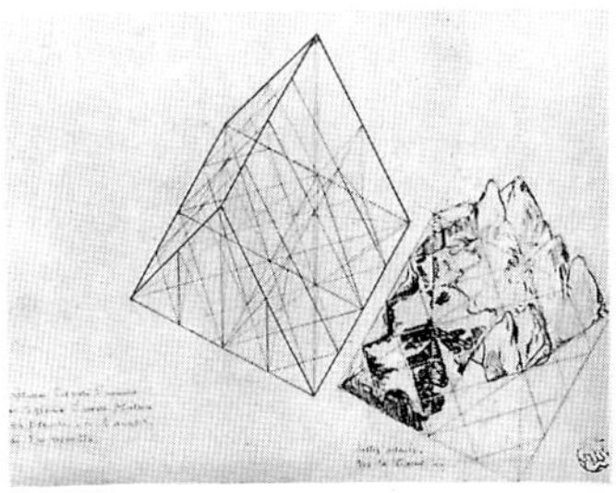

Mont-Blanc. Etude sur la constitution géodesique, sur ses transformations et sur l'état ancien et moderne de ses glaciers". The book is illustrated by a more complete series of diagrams than Ruskin's, showing step by step how the initially compact, prismatic volumes of the structure of the mountain were transformed into sharp, lacy and eroded contours, and how their form was sculpted by "streams or gradual weathering", by movement through "excavation", by subtracting mass or by "accumulation" — in other words the addition of mass.

LIKE Ruskin, Viollet-Le-Duc saw in the Alps a paradigm about form, structure, and movement, rather than an isolated story about the shaping of a single object. The paradigm was intended not only to explain the morphology of any region or any natural object, but was also meant to apply to any artifact, regardless of scale. Both Ruskin and Viollet-Le-Duc were interested in truth within design, believing that nature could demonstrate how the form of the structure of mountains was created directly by movement, without any other intervention.

THE paradigm of the Alps, however, was not easy to apply in practice. Both in nature and in design, it is rather rare to find objects whose structure is, or can be, formed by "sculpting". One of these rare cases is Leonardo da Vinci's method for creating the profile of bastions (streamlining of the line of fire, so to speak, or the contour of the fortification). In fact, Leonardo

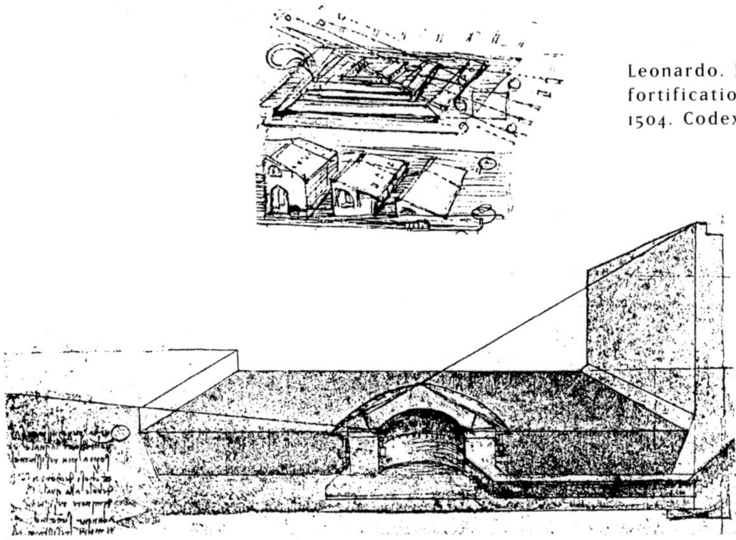

Leonardo. Representation of fortification and ballistic lines. c. 1504. Codex Atlanticus. f. 41. (v-a).

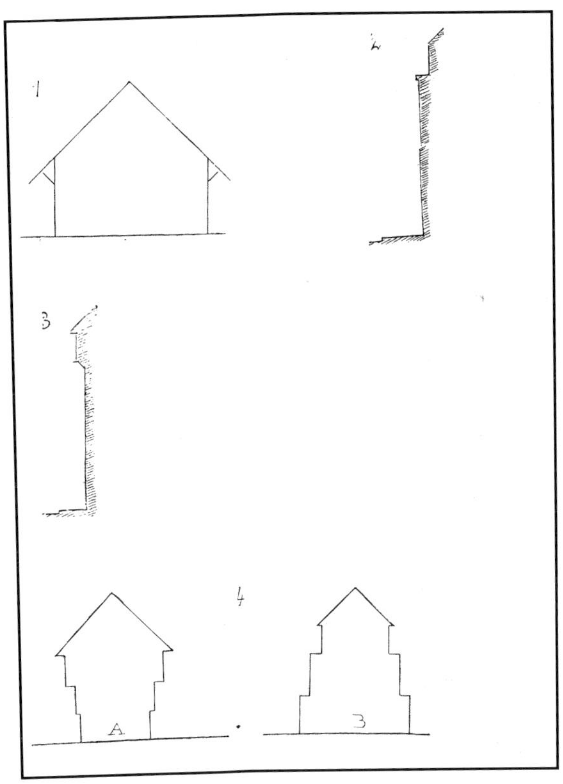

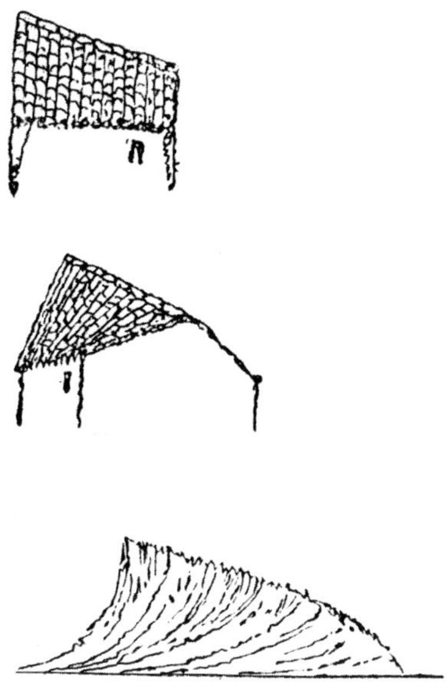

Ruskin's comparison between mountain ridges and house gables. Both from the region of the Alps. From his Modern Architecture. The Swiss Hut, from Viollet-le-Duc, Entretiens sur l'architecture.

struggled with the problem of selecting the correct form for canal subsidiaries, finding guidance in the empirical study of dendritic ramifications. But at that time, the conceptual or experimental tools for drawing conclusions based on tree-branching for channeling the movement of water were not available.

SUCH tools exist today, although their application is mostly limited to hydraulic, mechanical and traffic design. In these cases, structure forms a channel for a specific kind of movement. As we have seen, in Calatrava's infrastructure facilities, flow requirements dictate the dimensions, curve and convergent angle of the channel, in order to promote minimum "friction".

ALONG with Viollet-Le-Duc, Ruskin only produced one convincing application to architecture, namely the shape of the roof of a building as determined by the climate of the region, with the movement of water and snow envisioned as an analogy of the movement of glaciers shaping the Alps.

DESPITE these limitations of direct applicability, the paradigm of the Alps had an enormous impact in focusing designers' interest on the relationship between generative process and product, or the form of structures and their generative movement. For Ruskin, the memory of the generative process was a value. Memory was one of the seven "lamps of architecture". It had an emotional as well as cognitive importance. Looking back over life's past hours was a source of "peculiar gratitude". Additionally, Ruskin's writings on design and memory, which were later to have a major influence on Proust, assign a moral value to memory. Furthermore, his studies into the genesis of the Alps were a major stimulus to the birth of a new branch of research, described by Ruskin in his "Modern Painters" as the problem of "growth and form" — "morphogenesis" would be the term used by natural scientists — and thus pre-empting D'Arcy Thompson. Once this new approach had emerged, other more subtle and intricate relationships between structure and movement could be identified, promising new and unexplored frontiers for the world of design.

STRUCTURES that preserve in their form the memory of the movements that generated them — in the same way that the Alps have emerged out of streamlining, in the literal sense of the term — can be described as recording the movements that produced them "negatively"; in other words, these structures record the removal of material that reduces a complex and complete configuration down to a leaner version. Nevertheless, other methods are available for preserving memory. These methods "positively" record the movements that have produced structures through the assembly of material into a more complex and complete structure.

ONE way of preserving memory has been to leave part of the generic process unfinished — in a state of "non finito"[21], as aesthetics came to categorise the method. In the evolution of aesthetics, the notion of the unfinished as something positive has a long past, with its roots in the classical humanist poetics. A number of concepts express this idea; "non finito" is the most explicit, but there is also "sprezzatura", (a term introduced in Baldassare Castiglione's "Il libro del cortegiano" of 1528 and used in the Renaissance from about the same period as "non finito") and "negligence" from the 18th century. These concepts suggest that, far from leading to failure, the non-attainment of an absolute design goal, or the condonation of anomalies and rule violations, can be beneficial, bringing a sense of surprise, originality, vitality and openness, but most importantly, the memory of the creative moment.

MICHELANGELO appears to have been

21. J.A. Schmoll (Ed.), *Das Unvollendete als Künstlerische Form*, Bern 1959.

22. A. Condivi, *Michelangelo. La vita raccolta dal suo discepolo Ascani Condivi*, ed. by A. Maraini, Florence, 1928. Cited in David Summers, *Michelangelo and the Language of Art*, Princeton, p. 406.

greatly preoccupied with non finito. Many of his sculptures are suspended between rough stone and human form, the body or the face of a person barely emerging from the mass of the unworked material. The most famous examples of this idea are the slaves for the tomb of Julius II.

MANY reasons for his attachment to non finito have been suggested: one involves the crisis of neo-platonism, and another is political. In addition, Michelangelo despised non-legitimate claims to authority, and non finito was a form of criticism. He lived in a period of massive violence and deception which stemmed from authority. Thus, by definition, he was suspicious about any attempt at perfection and order. Additionally, his personality was demanding, contemplative and melancholy. He was wary of easy victory. He was unsympathetic to the idea of a human artifact achieving the status of perfection, lacking nothing. The same can be said not only for many other artists, but also for writers like Montaigne, a contemporary of Michelangelo, whose unfinished form was manifested in the clearly critical role of the syntax and semantic organisation of the text.

YET in addition to this critical role, non finito may have an other meaning: Argan and others have argued that the non finito in Michelangelo's work was probably part of his general preoccupation with movement which, as we know from Condivi's "Vita di Michelangelo"[22] of 1553, was the subject of a treatise planned by the artist. Movement preoccupied Michelangelo not only in its most narrow sense, namely the representation of moving bodies, but also with regard to the representation of the process of creation. Although a sculpture may have represented a person, and its unfinished fuzzy edge may have be represented the blurred outline of a figure in movement, it also represented generative movement, in other words the process of "a figure coming to life"; a figure "growing larger as the stone grows small", as Michelangelo himself described in his poem "Sicome per levar".

IN building, non finito as a means of recording generic movement in construction appears to have preoccupied the architects of antiquity. On some of the walls of the Propylaea of Athens, the ancones, knobs of stone or handling bosses (otherwise known as parotides, ota or katavoleis) used for raising and positioning the monumental masonry blocks still protude. According to one theory, due to a lack of funds they are simply there as part of an unfinished construction. But another claims that, as with the unfinished stone of Michelangelo's sculpture, they have been left on the structure intentionally, as a purposeful reminder of the generative movements such as the crafty use of hoists and levers during the building, and more importantly perhaps, the intelligence and the communal effort involved in bringing about what its creators saw as a unique structure. This is not implausible. After all, elements of classical architecture such as dentils, mutule, taeniae, gutuae and triglyphs are most frequently associated with more ancient wooden constructional methods which preceded stone, thus preserving their memory. Why not commemorate the movements involved in the erection and assembly of specific propylaea?

THERE is no such ambiguity in the famous "beton brut" of Le Corbusier's Unité d'Habitation. The concrete of the structure was explicitly left bare in order to conserve the wavy grain patterns, the intricate

SUSPENDED BETWEEN ROUGH STONE AND HUMAN FORM, ... A FORM OF CRITICISM. ...ABOUT ANY ATTEMPT AT PERFECTION AND ORDER.

Michelangelo. Awakening Slave. Galleria dell'Accademia. Florence.

THE CONCRETE OF THE STRUCTURE WAS EXPLICITLY LEFT BARE... A TESTIMONY OF MOVEMENT, RECALLING THE LIVELINESS OF THE HANDS AND MINDS OF THOSE WHO CREATIVELY APPLIED THE TECHNOLOGY OF THE TIMES.

arrangements of the fibers, the ribbons of tissue and the cracks or fissures — the inside face of the wooden shuttering planks on its exposed rough surface. This coarseness offended many critics at the time. Some saw Corbusier's refusal to conceal the crudeness and defects of the material simply as a pragmatic submission of the architect to the constraints imposed by post-war austerity.

THE intention, however, was quite different: Corbusier called these remnant wooden traces "wrinkles and birthmarks", and used them to create an aesthetic effect, or "contrast". With their "crudity", "intensity" and "spontaneity", they juxtaposed the extreme accuracy, detail and perfection of modern construction technology. Beyond the experience of aesthetic contrast, the preservation of these defects — these "wrinkles and birthmarks" — appears to be a testimony of movement, recalling the liveliness of the hands and minds of those who creatively applied the technology of the times. In fact, the very terms Le Corbusier used, namely "wrinkles" and "birthmarks", are signs of the passage of time on the human body, a part of his growth and aging. As with ancones protruding from the masonry structure of propylaea, these remnants were intended as witnesses of the structure's construction, the generative movement.

23. John Ruskin, *The Seven Lamps of Architecture*, New York 1961, p. 169.

THE rough, mottled, unpolished appearance, both of the propylaea of the Acropolis, in Athens, and the Unité d'Habitation, in Marseilles, is not an error. It has a specific meaning. They are what Ruskin called "shadows", through which structures find a "deep sense of voicefulness", a "mysterious sympathy" with the "passing waves of humanity". Their unfinished quality implies the effects of passing time and action. It provides the means through which structures record their own history, and memorise the movement that brought them about[23].

APART from the use of imperfect details, fragments, and unpolished surfaces, are there any methods by which generative movement can be embodied in a structure? Apart from the usual non finito methods, which mostly imprint onto the structure's skin, how can the history of the dynamic processes of a product's genesis be incorporated into its static form? For many designers, the idea of perfection, regardless of reason, continues to be unacceptable — Calatrava has never felt attracted by it.

Morphogenetic Movement

THE relationship between the process of construction, generative movement and the final form of a structure has been of major interest to philosophers, natural scientists, and biologists alike. Ideas go back to antiquity, when the morphology of organisms had been a subject of serious and intensive investigation. In his embryology, Aristotle, with very little empirical evidence, argued that "things formed by nature", as well as those formed "by human art", require in their making both movement (kinesis) and activity (energia). An animal, he observed, "comes into being" through a process which biologists now call morphogenesis, which resembles the "building of a house" in that it involves the action and movement of "some agency", thus causing the form of the animal to materialise in the womb[24].

IN his classic 20th century work "On Growth and Form"[25] (echoing Ruskin's phrase), the great British scientist and pioneer of the systematic study of the generation of the form of organisms, D'Arcy Thompson, makes the same point as Aristotle: the form of a structure is the product of a movement. With D'Arcy Thompson, however, the idea is based on extensive data, gained from observations and tests. The form of matter, he states in the introduction to his book, "whether living or dead", is the product of movement. Throughout the work, the configuration of organisms is studied in terms of movements which contribute to the "conformation" of their structure.

24. *Aristotle, Generation of Animals*, translated by A.L. Peck, Cambridge 1942.

25. D'Arcy Wentworth Thompson, *On Growth and Form*, The Complete Revised Edition, New York 1992. (First published 1942).

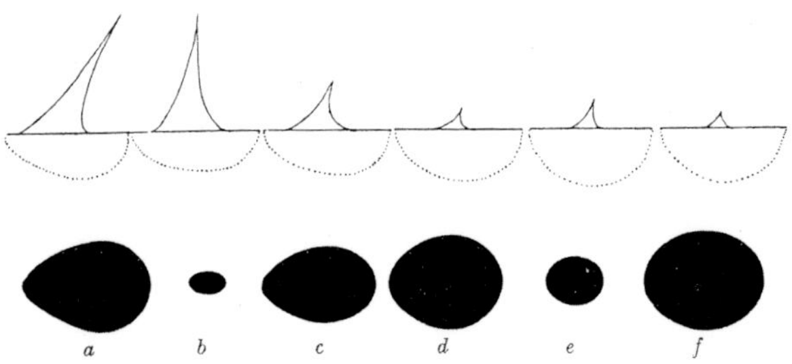

D'Arcy Wentworth Thompson, On Growth and Form, Cambridge, 1942. Typical forms of bird's eggs; a) green glover; b) humming bird; c) crow; d) pheasant; e) kingfisher; f) owl

ONE of the book's most well argued chapters is devoted to the origin of the shape of eggs. Although recent studies have empirically shown that the theory is wrong, it nevertheless serves as a conceptual framework for further investigations into the origins of shape with regard to a whole class of hollow structures — both natural and artificial — that are the products of peristaltic movement and "streamlining". The concept of streamlining has already been encountered during our discussion of 19th century theories on the origin of the profile and shape of the Alps, sculpted by movement. With D'Arcy Thompson's hollow structures, however, movement does not cause new structures of "living substance" to "conform" through the reduction of a more complete structure into simple rubble, as in the case of the Alps; rather, movement "impresses" form on structure by means of an intricate process "very much as we may wrap an apple in a handkerchief, hold the two ends fast, and twirl the apple round." Moreover, throughout Growth and Form, movement generally develops more complete and complex structures from elementary components of a "very simple kind" — the opposite to Ruskin, where form is produced by movement.

FOR contemporary biologists, the study of the phenomenon of development of organisms centres on three constructive processes: growth, morphogenesis and differentiation. Growth implies an increase in the size, mass and weight, through the process of addition; in other words, the production of protoplasm — the new stuff from which life is made. The term morphogenesis denotes the changes that take place in the organisation of a structure: new shapes; the spatial relationship of parts; splitting; the hollowing out and folding of matter. Differentiation, on the other hand, involves the diversification of a structure's morphology by form and function. In all three processes, and in particular with morphogenesis, structure emerges out of movement. Accordingly, it might be claimed that the form of the emerging structure directly embodies the movement that generated it or, metaphorically speaking, that the form of the structure retains the memory of the generative movement. This claim by D'Arcy Thompson is indeed extreme; it overstresses the environmental and mechanical factors, while disregarding hereditary and controlling factors, and the genetic mechanisms that determine movement. Nevertheless, D'Arcy Thompson has once again provided a paradigm for examining the relationship between structure and generative movement that will be valid for decades to come.

WITH regard to the new structure of artifacts, it is not difficult to assess the applicability of this discussion to the development of form. Artifacts emerge out of movements that add, transport, aggregate, split, hollow and fold the material from which they are made, while developing through growth, the evolution of new forms and the differentiation of parts. As a result, generative movements become embodied in the configuration of these artifacts; applicable to both organisms and artifacts, we shall refer collectively to all three kinds of movements as "morphogenetic movement".

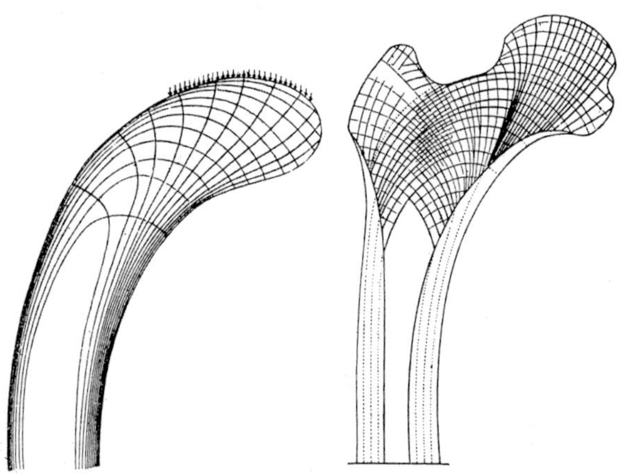

D'Arcy Wentworth Thompson. Crane head and femur.

AS with the configuration of the structure of organisms, so with that of artifacts: the structure emerges not only from morphogenetic movement but also from the instructions that control these movements — instructions that are hereditary, and precede the morphogenesis. These instructions (supplied by genes in the case of organisms, and constructional plans in the case of artifacts) are themselves the product of a long evolution and a movement that involves the searching and testing of alternatives, with the processing of the resultant information ultimately leading to a new type of structure. The structural form of an organism or artifact not only incorporates the morphogenetic movements that acted upon it during the short period during which the new individual structure was produced, but also those movements that took place during the evolution — or history of emergence — of the structure's type. With regard to the conservation of the memory of movements, therefore, we can conclude that the form of such structures is the outcome of evolution or history. This implies movement that took place over an extended period of time.

THE products of this evolution or history have already been referred to as well-formed, complex structures. Whether pertaining to organisms or artifacts, these structures are successful survivors: while sustaining a multitude of loads and transmitting them to the ground without detriment, and appearing to do so with the minimum of resources, they have succeeded in achieving a state of equilibrium. The complexity of their form is related to their evolution or history — an accumulation of modifications to the structure's form. Leaving aside issues of teleology and entelechy in evolution or history, each modification appears to be a response to numerous threatening load conditions, involving the opportune movement of matter in order to overcome force aggressions while arranging matter more efficiently, strengthening the structure where most necessary (across the lines of internal forces), responding to concentrations of tensile stress or dispensing with superfluous material. Gradually, a well-formed structure will be produced in which, according to Galileo in the "Dialogues Concerning the Two New Sciences" of 1638: "the superfluous material has been removed" offering "the same resistance (strength) at all points".

AS far as organisms are concerned, this will explain the scarcity of orthological, uniform, cross-sectional, post-and-beam structures which fail to exhibit an efficient and effective allocation of material. Of course, in the case of buildings, there is a reason for choosing such structurally inefficient or ineffective shapes: orthological, uniform, post-and-beam structures are generally more beneficial to use, production and transportation. Nevertheless, there are designers who, while aiming to achieve well-formed structures, will systematically chose intricate, "organic" and dynamic shapes for their projects — and even their building projects. Santiago Calatrava is such a designer.

STRUCTURES abound in Calatrava's work that are typified by highly articulated members which, like organisms, possess rounded corners and avoid abrupt, sectional contrasts. His designs possess sections that adapt to varying bending moments; his columns are broader in their middle, and taper gradually towards both ends. Most frequent in his work is the use of highly differentiated elements, composed of non-uniform materials, where each material — again like the members of organisms — assumes the task it can best perform. Typical in Calatrava's work is the non-orthogonal allocation of structural members to eliminate the detouring of forces, directing them down to earth by the shortest path.

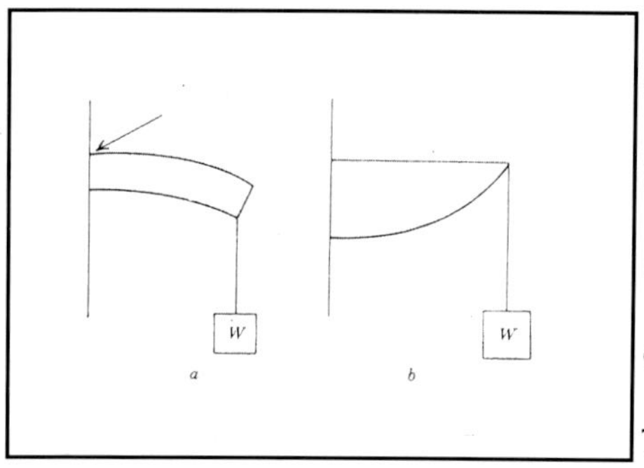

D'Arcy Wentworth Thompson.
Girder Outlines.

THE memory of the generative movements which took place in the evolution or history of Calatrava's structural forms is thus preserved in striking contrast to non finito;

while non finito leaves direct but superficial traces of movement, with Calatrava, the developmental processes of growth, morphogenesis and differentiation preserve that movement within the actual configuration of the structure's body.

BUT having seen how movement leaves its mark on a structure, a further step can be taken: by examining the past of a structure, its future — or possible future — can be revealed. The form of a given structure implies movement; not movement which has already occurred, but movement which may occur, potential movement.

Morphogenetic Movement

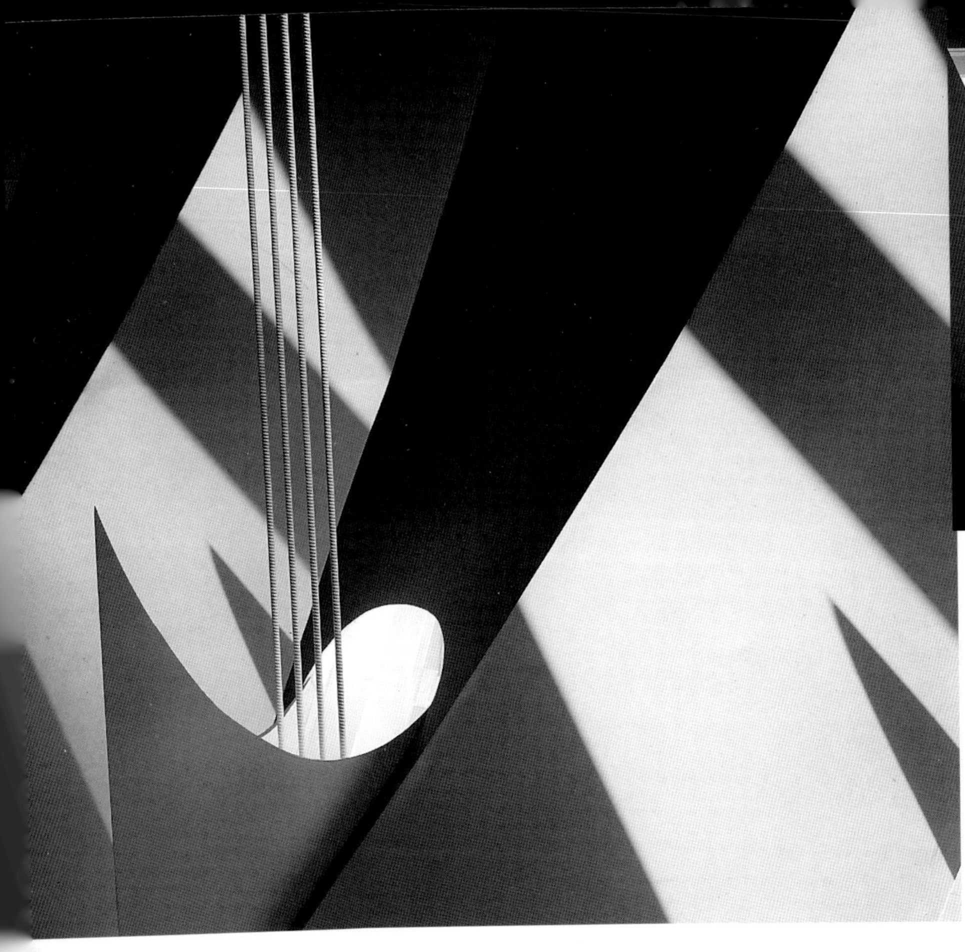

Bärenmatte Community Centre

STRUCTURES ABOUND IN CALATRAVA'S WORK THAT ARE TYPIFIED BY HIGHLY ARTICULATED MEMBERS WHICH, LIKE ORGANISMS, POSSESS ROUNDED CORNERS AND AVOID ABRUPT, SECTIONAL CONTRASTS. HIS DESIGNS POSSESS SECTIONS THAT ADAPT TO VARYING BENDING MOMENTS; HIS COLUMNS ARE BROADER IN THEIR MIDDLE, AND TAPER GRADUALLY TOWARDS BOTH ENDS. MOST FREQUENT IN HIS WORK IS THE USE OF HIGHLY DIFFERENTIATED ELEMENTS, COMPOSED OF NON-UNIFORM MATERIALS, WHERE EACH MATERIAL — AGAIN LIKE THE MEMBERS OF ORGANISMS — ASSUMES THE TASK IT CAN BEST PERFORM.

Bärenmatte Community Centre

Morphogenetic Movement

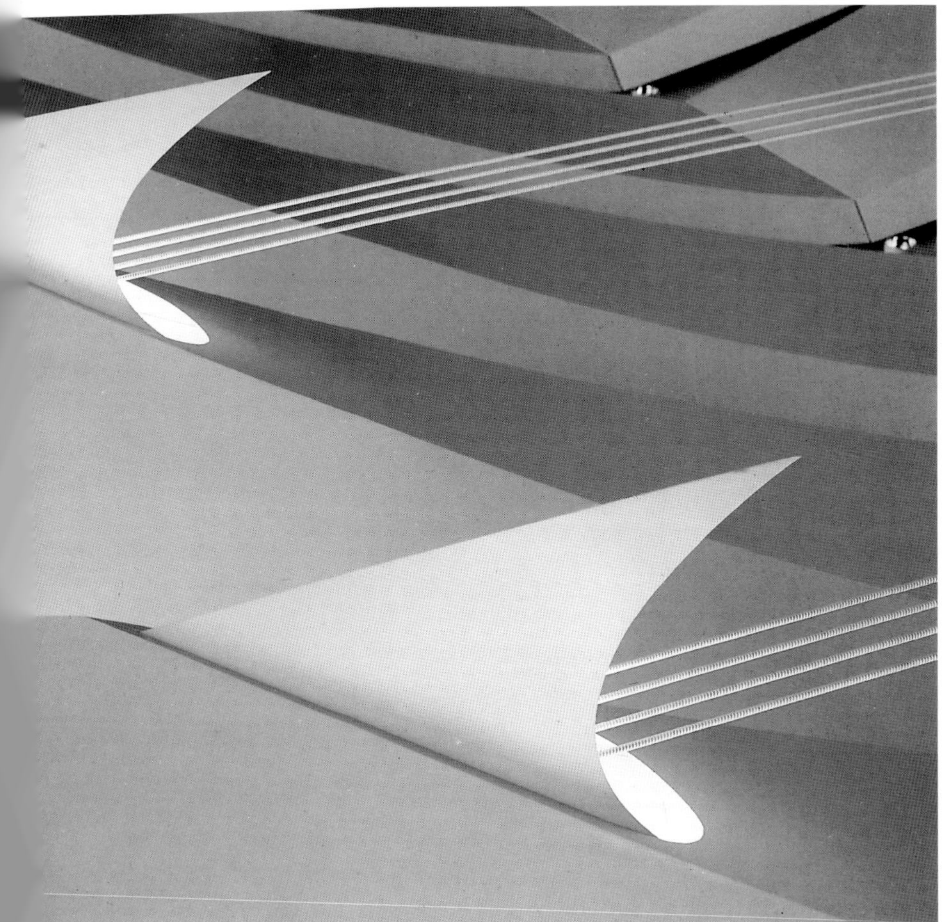

THE erection of a structure calls for the movement of materials. But what makes those materials move? A satisfactory scientific explanation has been available at least since Galileo and Newton, involving the key concepts of force, energy and work. In order to move a given material, a force has to act upon it. Energy — so-called kinetic energy — has to be supplied; work has to be done.

BUT once this material has been moved, or raised into place, how does it stop moving? What, in other words, prevents its collapse? What has happened to the energy that moved it? Once again, Newton provides the answer: a structure does not move because of its balanced configuration (which can be defined as the distribution of a structure's mass, whereby any force related to the structure is opposed by an equal one). In any standing structure, it is therefore possible to envisage a diagram of forces and counter forces. To turn once more to D'Arcy Thompson: "The form of an object is a diagram of forces". In the final analysis, for D'Arcy Thompson morphology "is not only a study of material things and the forms of material things, but its dynamic aspect ...the interpretation, in terms of force, and the operations of energy" (p.19). "In an organism", he stated, "great or small, it is not merely the nature of the motions of the living substance which we must interpret in terms of force (according to kinetics), but also the conformation of the organism itself, whose permanence or equilibrium is explained by the interaction or balance of forces, as described in statics".

NEVERTHELESS, we can envision in a structure more than just a diagram of forces. The energy supplied to raise up the structure's material is not lost; it has been stored in the structure, in the relative position of the material distributed within the structure's configuration. It has become what is referred to as "potential energy", meaning that, under certain conditions, it can revert to kinetic energy — which in turn will lead to movement. The form of a structure, therefore, is a diagram not only of acting and counteracting forces, but also of potential energy, and of the ability of the body of the structure to move under specific circumstances. The form of a structure, then, is a kind of map of virtual movement. Calatrava has clearly voiced his fascination with virtual kinematics: "Strength", he has said, "both in architecture and in mechanics, is equal to mass times acceleration. Mass is an abstract universal unit, which means that mobility is implicit in the concept of strength. A simple way of translating this is to say that strength can be likened to crystallised movement." How, then, can this virtual movement become actual?

A STRUCTURE will remain standing because it is maintained in a state of equilibrium. Every external force that appears, to threaten it, will be resisted by another, equal force. What, then, will happen if any of these resisting forces are removed through alteration of the structure? What will happen if some previously controlled forces are set free, to act upon the material? At what point will the potential energy stored both in the mass and the position of the structure's material be unleashed, to once more become kinetic energy? The simple answer is that some components of the structure will start to move. The nature of the movement, and its degree of devastation, will depend on how the material is distributed and interlocked within the structure; in other words, on the way it has been moved, lifted into position and assembled. The structure may disintegrate gradually; it may, on the other hand, collapse in its entirety, to totally destroy either organism or artifact.

IT is thus clear that, in examining a structure's configuration, it is possible to envisage not only the movements involved in its erection, but also its disassembly. In this respect, a structure can relate to movement not only through preservation of the memory of its probable construction, but also projection of the image of its eventual destruction — generation and catastrophe, hand in hand.

IS it strange to relate structures to movement in such an unraveling, "unpacking" way? Is it perverse, or adversarial? On the contrary, to encourage visions of stable structures as they are transformed into a collection of moving parts will heighten our awareness of the potential movement locked within structures, which can in turn lead to ideas for possible new structures, enhanced problem solving, or an invitation to dream-work.

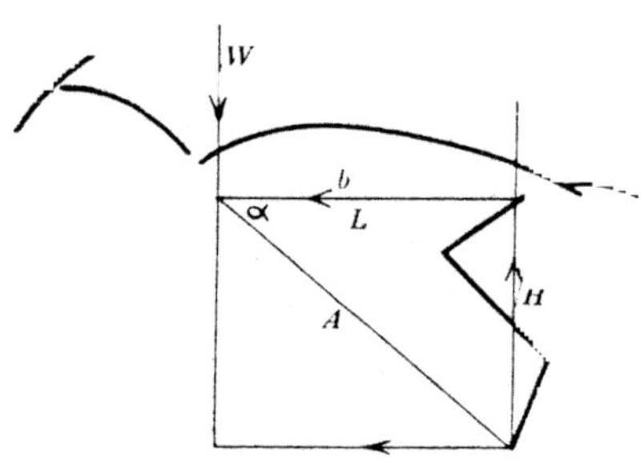

D'Arcy Wentworth Thompson.
Representation of a horse in motion.

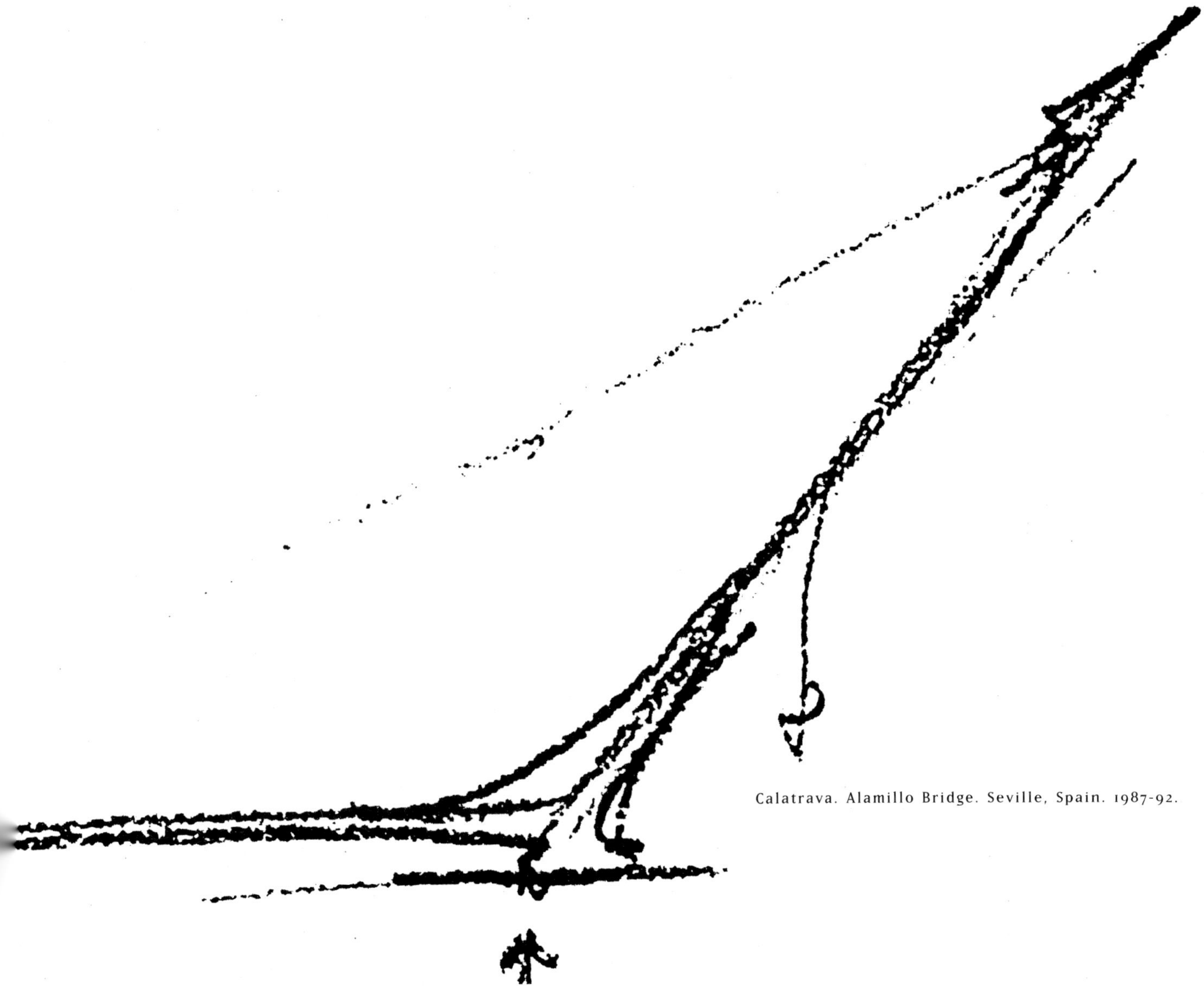

Calatrava. Alamillo Bridge. Seville, Spain. 1987-92.

SINCE antiquity, critics and commentators of art have associated movement in painting and in sculpture with the breaking of planar conventions or the denial of compositional limits. The idea of "progress" in the art of Ancient Greece has been equated with the gradual disengagement of the limbs from the simple pillar-like "block" structure of the human body, in other words the realistic representation of movement arising through a corresponding modular decomposition of structure. This development commences with the kouroi, sculpted with "one foot brought forth", and continues to the gods, who have their arms bent and turned forward. Finally, divinities and athletes assume the most articulated and complex positions, where all members of the body appear as if torn from the torso, to become engaged in the most "lively", "elaborate" and even "violent" acts — the terms used by Quintilian, the Roman theoretician of rhetoric and aesthetics, in describing the attitude of Discobolos of Myron, the daring sculptor famous for his expression of movement in antiquity[26].

26. Quintilian, Institutio Oratoria, translated by H.E. Butler, Cambridge 1980 (1920).

THE actual disengagement of members from the human body from the primitive block, and the resulting arrangement of compositional components in order to achieve a sense of movement, were not arbitrary, but carefully composed and systematically codified by the sculptor Policlitos in his book "The Canon", written in the 5th century BC. We do not know the exact content of the Policlitos book, which has been lost, but we are told by later authors that he prescribed the structure of the human body as resting on one leg, pushed a little to the rear, with the other leg bent at the knee and applying

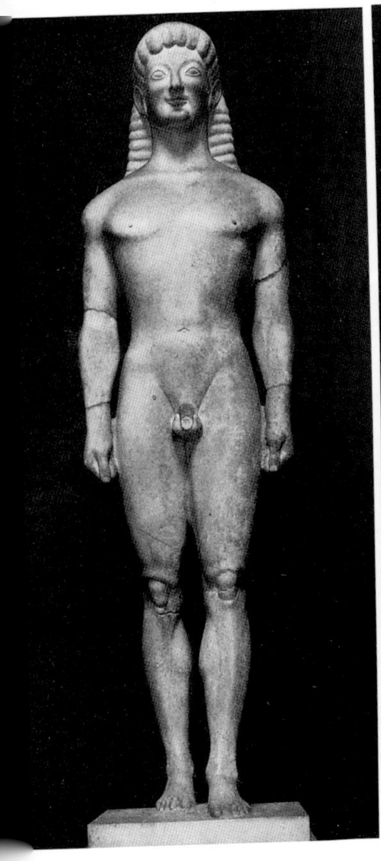

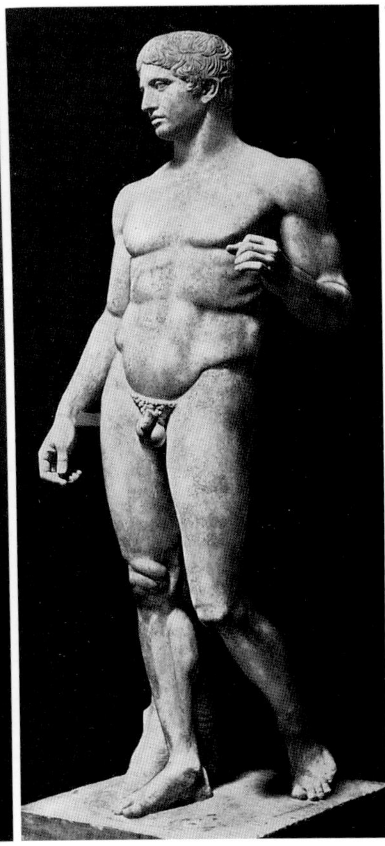

THE IDEA OF "PROGRESS" IN THE ART OF ANCIENT GREECE HAS BEEN EQUATED WITH THE GRADUAL DISENGAGEMENT OF THE LIMBS FROM THE SIMPLE PILLAR-LIKE "BLOCK" STRUCTURE OF THE HUMAN BODY, IN OTHER WORDS THE REALISTIC REPRESENTATION OF MOVEMENT ARISING THROUGH A CORRESPONDING MODULAR DECOMPOSITION OF STRUCTURE

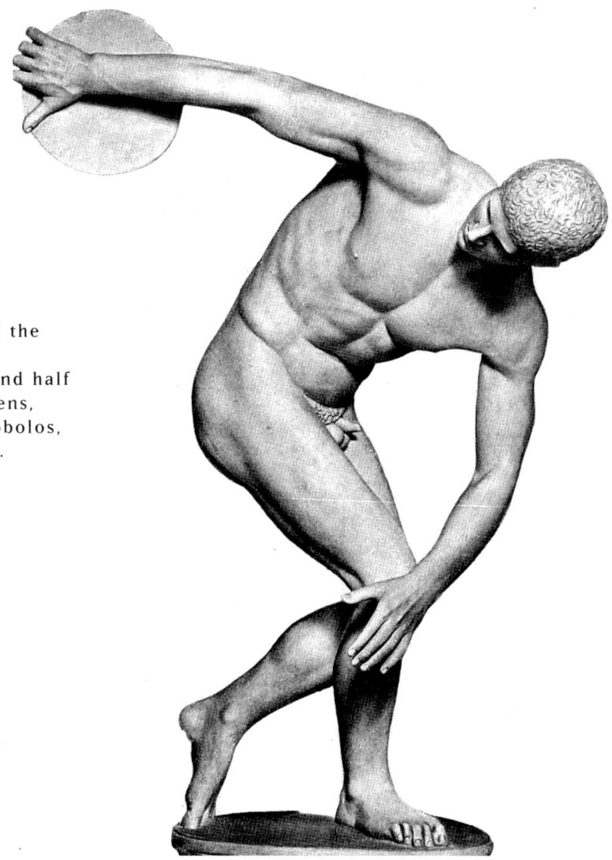

Kouros from Tegea, first part of the 4th century BC. Munich; the Diadoumenos of Policlitos, second half of the 5th century BC. Copy Athens, National Museum; Myron's Discobolos, mid-4th century BC. Copy. Rome.

less pressure. The chest, while tilted backwards, was slightly bent also, and the head leaned to the side in the opposite direction to the chest. This "counter posing" of the members of the body was seen as a way of expressing graceful movement, a quality Policlitos' sculptures were praised for.

CLEARLY, Policlitos did not provide instructions for depicting the image of specific, real-life moving bodies. As indicated by the very concept of The Canon, he created an abstract system of rules based on axes, and a set of relationships between them. It was a powerful framework, able to capture the most significant characteristics of any kind of human body in motion and, as we shall later see, applicable to the representation of any kind of structure.

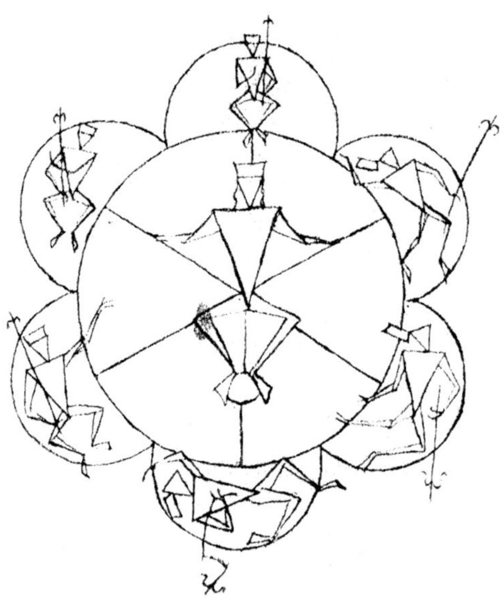

Villard de Honnecourt. "The Wheel of Fortune", from Sketchbook of Villard de Honnecourt, edited by Th. Bowie. Bloomington, 1959. p. 139.

A THEORY, probably similar to Policlitos', on the representation of the moving body can be found in the Villard de Honnecourt's famous thirteenth century sketchbook (Plate 64), which he himself titled the "Wheel of Fortune". The body and its members are represented by means of axes. Next to the image, Villard writes: "Here below are the figures of the Wheel of Fortune ...seven of them...". A large figure in the sitting position, with legs apart and arms open, occupies the centre of the page. It is depicted within a circle, and strictly symmetrical. The figure wears a crown, and is surrounded by six other figures, smaller in size, although identically articulated through the convention of axes. The smaller figures are placed around the circle to create a kind of hexagon pattern. Situated directly above the central figure is a sitting figure, with legs apart, forming a symmetrical pattern. Assuming a counter position, its arms breaking the symmetry, the left arm, supporting a sceptre, reaches down to rest on the leg. The right arm is slightly raised. Clockwise, the following figure has abandoned symmetry. The two arms are clearly counter positioned, the right being raised and the left lowered. The two legs turn and lean in the same direction. The body is no longer immobile like the previous figure; it appears to be moving, starting to fall. The crown is almost off the figure's head, yet the sceptre is still firmly grasped. The next figure is even more out of symmetry, and definitely stooping. The sceptre is now also raised. At the bottom of the illustration, the fifth figure has totally collapsed. And there is no longer any trace of symmetry. Arms and legs have assumed complete counter positions. The crown is off, and the sceptre is broken. In the next position, however, we see the figure returning to the sitting position and to symmetry. Finally, the figure has assumed the sitting position, and is almost symmetrical.

TAKEN as a whole, the illustration represents a combinatorial enumeration of the various key arrangements that are possible for the structure of the human body, with legs and arms sequenced between a fully bilateral symmetrical arrangement and a completely counter-positional arrangement. The illustration also appears to represent an order for the states of stability associated with alternative structural arrangements, either from complete stasis to final collapse or, conversely, from disjointed fragments to erection and equilibrium.

IN the sketchbook's standard edition, the illustration's circular pattern reappears just two plates later. Villard de Honnecourt annotates the drawing, mentioning that the wheel can "turn of its own accord", like the wheel of a perpetual motion machine. Indeed,

Villard boasts of knowing the "way to do it", employing "mullets" and "quicksilver," although he fails to provide any real details! Given the affinity and the proximity of the two drawings, we can speculate that, like the second illustration, the first is also a machine of some kind. Perhaps Villard believed that he could impart motion to the whole wheel by putting the little figures on its periphery into motion, in other words by sequentially changing the position of their body members. More likely, however, is that the diagram is an abstract model, of interest due to its systematic combinatorial character, and its demonstration of the way in which the symmetric and counter positional forms of a structure relate, both to each other and to movement. Like The Canon, it offers a conceptual framework for the representation of structure, stability and movement; a subject which certainly must have been of great interest to cathedral builders like Villard and his colleagues.

LEON Battista Alberti was also preoccupied with the representation of movement in human bodies. In his famous treatise "On Painting"[27], he is fascinated with the moving body. Although in its representation he saw a equivalent between the motion of a body and emotions — movements of the soul, documented "from nature" — the result was a very abstract system of combinatorics of body-disposition, based on the notion of "balance". Excessively violent movements, and extreme distortions of the body simultaneously showing back and front, were

27. Leon Battista Alberti, *On Painting and Sculpture*, The latin texts of *De Pictura and De Statua*. Edited with translations, introduction and notes by Cecil Grayson, London 1972. On contraposto, see *De Pictura*, III, p. 20.

28. Giovanni Paolo Lomazzo, *Trattato dell'arte della pittura* (1584).

29. Gotthold Ephraim Lessing, *Laocoon, an Essay upon the Limits of Painting and Poetry*, New York, 1957. (*Laokoon. Über die Grenzen der Malerei und Poesie*, 1766)

30. Anthony Ashley Cooper, Earl of Shaftesbury, *Characteristics*, New York 1964 (1711).

"The Flame". Kinetic sculpture by Calatrava.

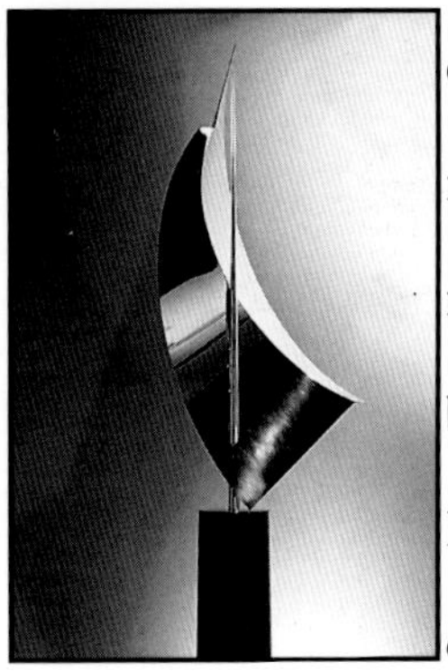

censured "as neither possible nor felicitous".

AFTER Alberti, interest in the representation of movement, including violent movement, increased. In the name of movement, so too did the appetite for exaggerated body positions. Nevertheless, the framework of Policlitos' The Canon remained the basic reference for discussing the problem. But there was now a concept for referring to this framework, namely "contraposto". Contraposto literally means "counter position" (a term we have already been using). Contraposto is the translation into Italian of the Greek word "antithesis", a term initially used in literature to refer to a family of forceful rhetorical means for the emphasis of a point using semantic or formal linguistic contrast. It is interesting that, in choosing this term, the Rennaissance theoreticians of design joined two modes of expression, and combined two traditions: on the one hand, the visual mode and the tradition of associating configuration with movement, according to The Canon, and on the other, the verbal mode and the tradition of associating a literary figure with a meaning, stemming from poetics.

FOR Giovanni Paolo Lomazzo (1584)[28] , contraposto, while borrowing from Alberti's treatment of body and movement, is more daring and abstract. For Lomazzo (here quoting Aristotle), no other form "expresses movement" better than that "of the flame of fire" which, he notes, resembles the form of the letter S. Alberti had also admired "spirals", but not for their "movements of animate beings". Lomazzo refers not to Alberti but to Michelangelo — who, as we have seen, was planning to write on the idea of movement — as the artist who preached the idea of the "serpent-like figure" ("figura serpentinata" as he calls this S-form), and applied it to the human body in particular, in order to empower it with movement. He quoted Michelangelo, who suggested the serpent-like line to achieve: "the greatest grace and loveliness that a figure may have", which was to him movement — the "furia" of a figure. Assuming that certain relationships between "length, breath and proportion of the limbs" are preserved, Lomazzo explains how the body can be arranged in a manner which, while destroying its symmetry, preserves its balance. In fact, the S-form is a very abstract, extreme schematisation of the contraposto of The Canon.

WHAT is interesting in these investigations into contraposto and the serpentine figure is that, although they represent the moving body, they are nevertheless abstract concepts applicable to any other object. They capture the moment when a structure, as if arrested by an invisible power, is poised in a state of equilibrium and immobility, on the brink of possible collapse. Beyond abstract homologies, however, this analogy between objects opens the way to dream-work and creative associations.

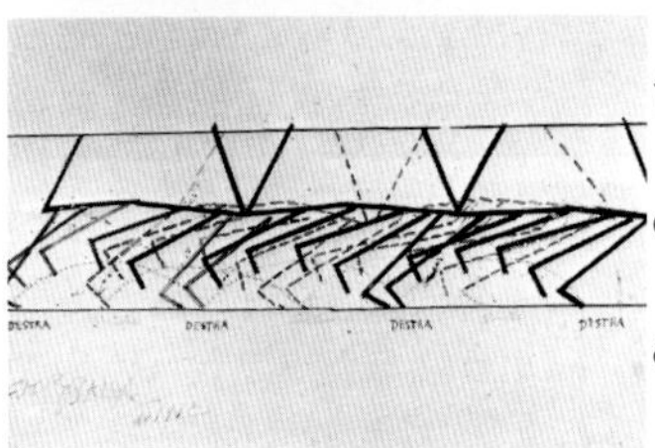

Giacomo Balla. 1912. Private collection.
Giacomo Balla. 1912. Milano. Galleria Civica d'Arte Moderna

GOTTHOLD Ephraim Lessing[29], already mentioned above, was the first to devote a book to the comparative representation of virtual movement in art and literature. Influenced by Shaftesbury, his book "Laocoon" considered the representation of action as one of the greatest challenges of both art as a whole and, in particular, the Laocoon complex — one of culture's greatest achievements.

The Laokoon.

TO quote Shaftesbury's "The Moralist": "New forms arise, when the old dissolve...a passage to some better world...a hidden scene of wonders, worlds within worlds...pregnant with more wonders...the abyss of space". Lessing was fascinated by the emergence of a new state out of the old, and the degree to which a representation could capture both states within a "pregnant" configuration. His idea was that the artist, as opposed to the writer "can use but a single moment of action...this single moment he makes as pregnant as possible", thus using Shaftsbury's expression. In this single moment, the "artist unites two distinct points of time". The compositions of the artist are "coexistent", they can "use only a single moment of an action, and must therefore choose ...the one most suggestive of what has occurred before and what is to follow". That they captured such a pregnant moment, and thus embodied movement, was the fascinating quality of the contraposto disposition and the serpentine line[30].

THE preoccupation with the paradox of the pregnant moment has distinguished Calatrava's designs from those of 1920s architects — architects who became fascinated by the representation of movement in their structures, implicitely in a single figure, like Eric Mendelsohn, or by means of multiple, adjacent poses clearly of the same figure, as with many artists within the cubist, futurist and constructivist movements. They were the equivalents of the work of photographers Eadward Muybridge and Etienne Jules Marey. More recently, Frank Gehry has attempted to capture movement in the same fractured, multifaceted way in his fragmented, overlapping architectural forms.

CALATRAVA is radically different: his work still follows the classical poetics of Policlitos, the Renaissance and Lessing, and latently represents — in a single moment and with singular ingenuity and intensity — both past and future states in the world of structures. Rarely has this been more clearly expressed than in Calatrava's sculpture of the S-shaped flame. In fact, few designers of structures have explored this concept, inorder to relate movement to structure in the same way that Calatrava has. Through his

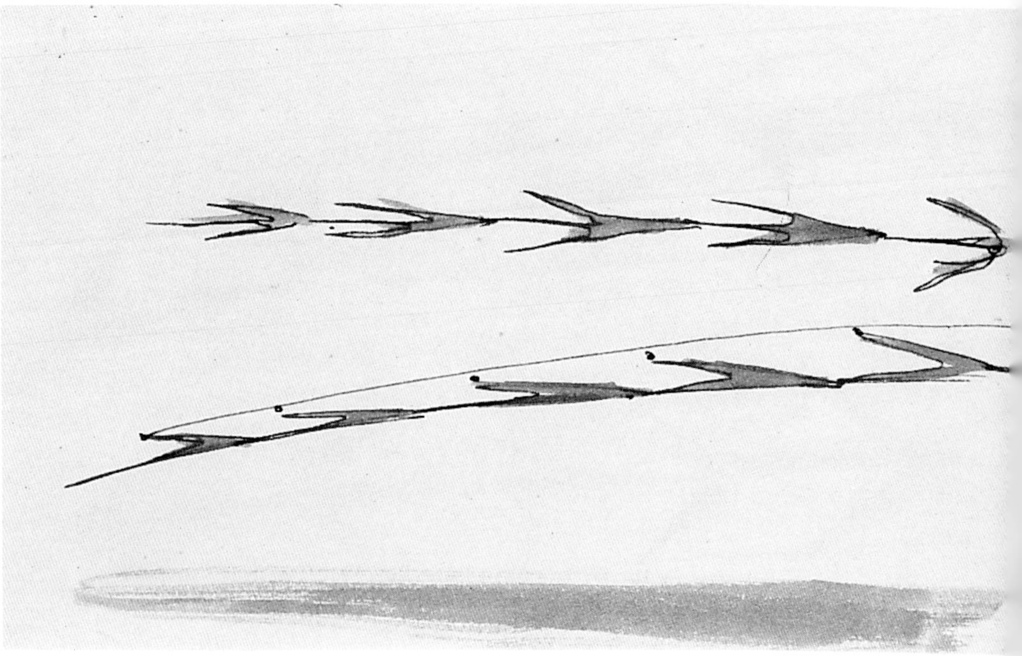

Calatrava drawing. Bridge study.

Movement of model airplane showing stall. Drawing made from a chronophotograph. 1890. CRAS. November 1891.

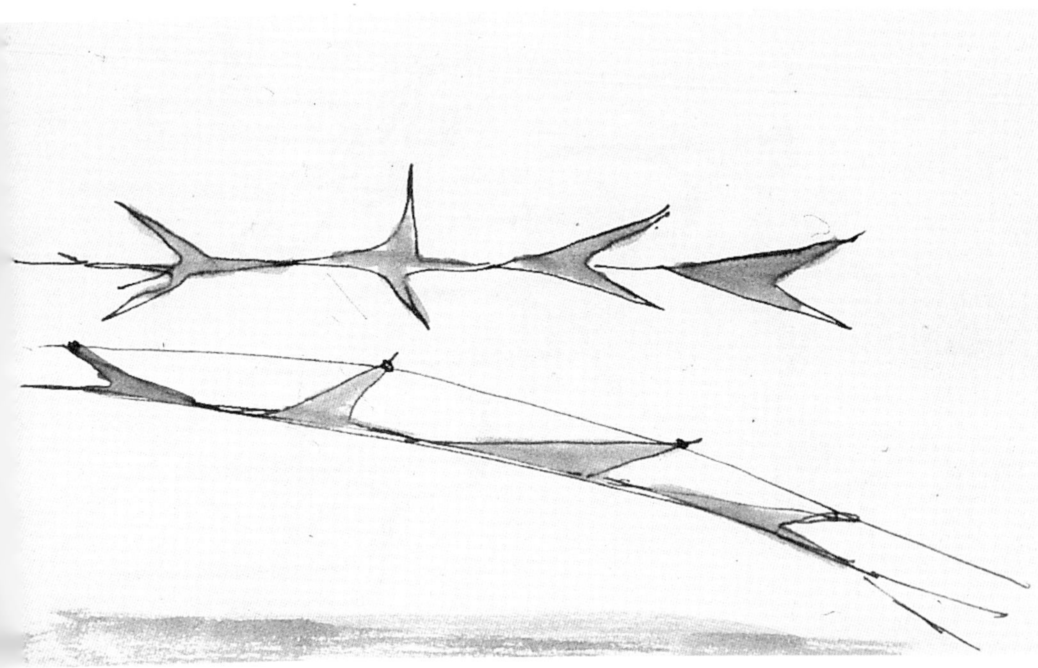

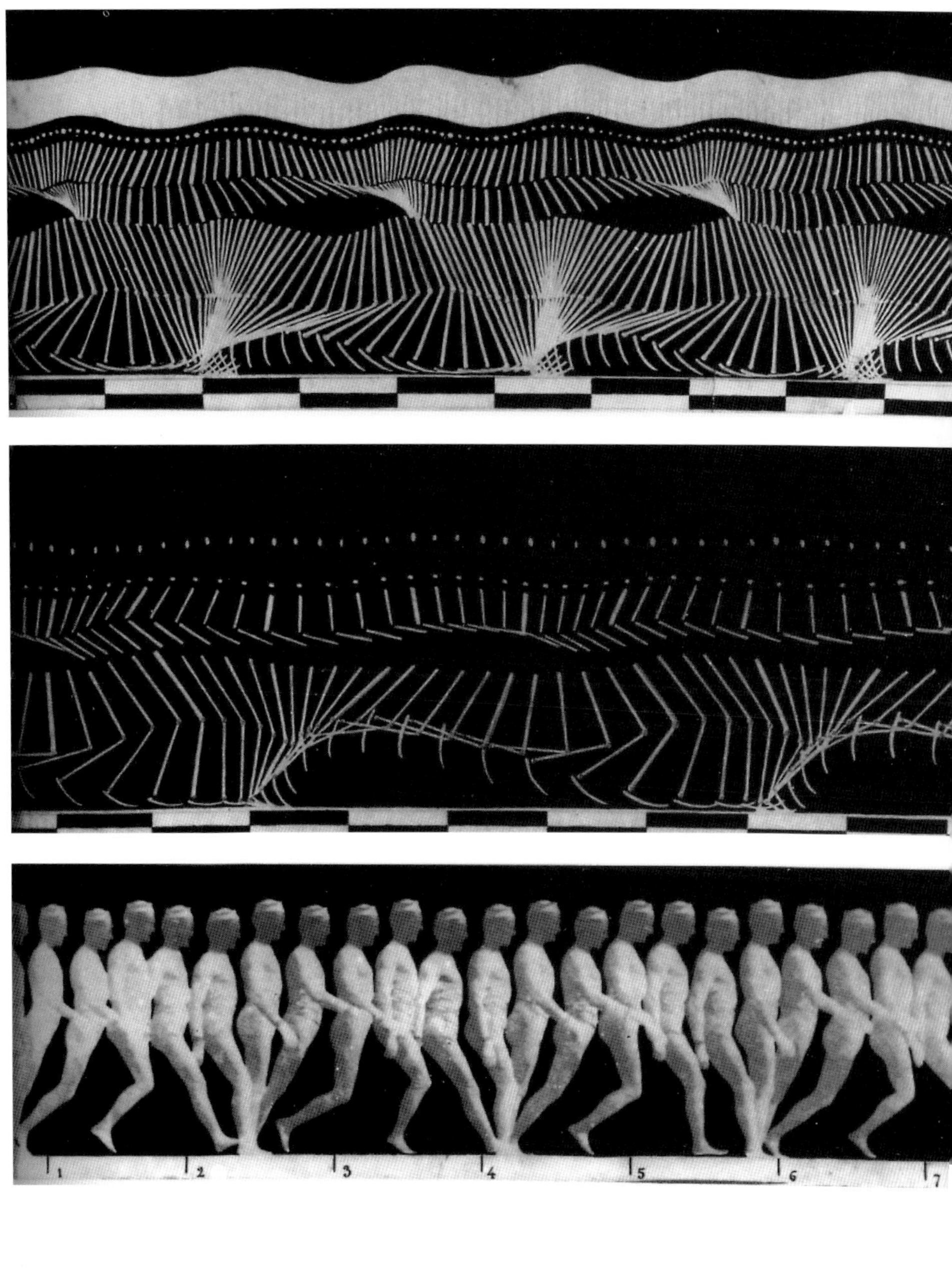

Etienne-Jules Marey, Photographic time study of a man dressed and nude in motion, 1886. Museum E.-J. Marey et des Beaux-Arts

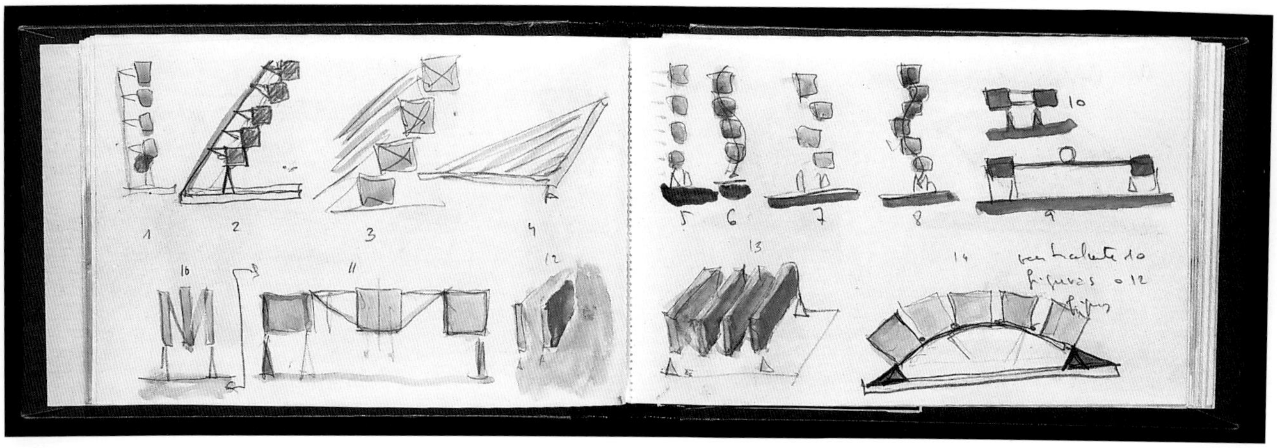

Alamillo Bridge

STRUCTURES, ALTHOUGH WHOLE, TO APPEAR AS ELEMENTS DESIGNED WITH CONTRADICTORY INTENTIONS. TO ENHANCE THIS EFFECT, CALATRAVA SEEMS TO INDULGE IN CONFIGURING THESE DELICATELY BALANCED, APPARENTLY OPPOSED MEMBERS AT THE ULTIMATE LIMIT OF RISK; HE APPEARS TO ADOPT A DESIGN STRATEGY THAT LINKS THE CONCEPT OF THE PREGNANT MOMENT IN AESTHETICS TO THE NOTION REFERRED TO BY ENGINEERS AS THE "CRITICAL POINT"

Pregnant Moment

Bach de Roda Bridge

reliance on the implicitness of the figure, Calatrava forces the viewer to reflect, contemplate and dream, and thus become a part of the creative process.

ONE of the dominant Calatrava motifs is the upright support which leans, to be arrested on the brink of falling — the motif of virtual movement, perhaps, or of structure at the threshold of catastrophe. Because it is restrained by tensioning elements, cables or strings, however, the support does not fall; indeed, more in the original contraposto spirit, in the absence of tensioning elements this apparently falling structure is either saved by developing a new version of the form — folding a member in the opposite direction for the purpose of counterbalancing, for example — or by differentiation of the structure through the addition of some other auxiliary element, to support it by acting in compression. As already mentioned, the idea of contrast here combines with the idea of juxtaposition in time. In appearing suspended between solid permanence and violent disappearance, the structure is thus "pregnant" with movement. It is also an "oxymoron" — a term used by theoreticians of poetics to describe a figure of speech that combines seemingly contradictory elements.

IT is common practice in the Calatrava oeuvre for structures, although whole, to appear as elements designed with contradictory intentions. To enhance this effect, Calatrava seems to indulge in configuring these delicately balanced, apparently opposed members at the ultimate limit of risk; he appears to adopt a design strategy that links the concept of the pregnant moment in aesthetics to the notion referred to by engineers as the "critical point" — the point beyond which, if a certain design variable is exceeded, the interatomic bonds of a member will be broken and the structure will disintegrate. Like an acrobat or a shrewd dancer, in concentrating loads around a critical point, slimming sections down to a critical dimension and raising of slope lines to a critical degree, Calatrava appears to revel in these apparently extreme structural conditions.

FAR from being sublime and arousing feelings of irrational fear, the effect of adopting — or apparently adopting — such critical conditions is cognitive. They stimulate reflection by means of an oxymoron; they shock, and give rise to wonder. The structure is falling, and yet it does not fall. Wonder leads to the search for an answer. As with D'Arcy Thompson, the envisagement of structural form as a diagram of operating forces and potential energy is actively encouraged — a diagram that derives its vividness from the articulated extremes of the structure's seemingly contradictory form.

HENCE, we can recognise the complex contraposto profile of the pergola supports at Stadelhofen Station, leaning to reach out, only to return — a theme recurring in different versions and scales in the Montjuic Communications tower, in the supports of St. John the Divine, in the Railway Station portico, in Lucerne and in the Tabourettli Theatre. And thus we sense the "pregnant moment" of the single arch of the La Devesa Bridge in Ripoll, swerving on the point of collapse, or the mast of the Trinity Bridge at Salford and the Bach de Roda Bridge in Barcelona. The above projects participate to some degree in all three qualities, as do the sculptures of the combinatoric games played with the floating cube or cubes, the suspension strings and long conic or conoid supports, the sculpture of the pecking bird or the perpetually moving eye.

THE implicit movement of the pregnant moment can be identified somewhere within the abstract composition of these physical structures. Within their tensioned or compressed components emerges the conceptual movement of the oxymoron, or even the idea of the virtual movement of the contraposto.

To reiterate: every structure, whether large or small, is a source of wonder for the onlooker. Of course, for the designer, this sense of wonder will begin at an earlier stage, with the enquiry into a structure's still unknown form: "What form should this structure take?" The answer is multilayered. In accordance with Leonardo da Vinci's principle that "the first and most important thing is stability (permanentia)" (Brit. Museum 138a), the solution can be a simple post-and-beam structure. With that, "what seemed to be a wonder", to again quote Stevin, "becomes wonder no more." The satisfaction derived from such a solution can indeed be brief. Along with the response to this "first level of design achievement", however, a new puzzle will emerge: the level of stability satisfaction, manifest in the question: "Is this the best design for the structure?" The designer may now embark on an identification of the movement of forces within the post-and-beam structure, detecting its inherently inefficient detouring of forces and undesirable moments. From this investigation, a new solution may emerge, giving new form to the structure by channelling its forces via the shortest path — subject to compression loads only, as with a parabolic arch — and thus minimising the costs associated with detouring. But once again, in responding on the second level of design achievement — the optimisation level, so to speak — new puzzles may emerge, involving tensional forces,

Calatrava. Tabourettli Theatre. Basel.

restrictions in use or structural span and weight. Further optimisation of the structure may follow: the introduction of loaded members such as trusses, a mixing of materials and, in the case of new configurations, even the replacement of traditional materials with a synthesis of new. Nevertheless, as a globally optimum design is approached, the sense of wonder may gradually seem to fade; to recall Mach, disillusionment may set in.

AT this point, the designer may turn to another assertion by Leonardo: "Voglio far miraculi!" (W.An.IV,167a) — "I want to create miracles!". This represents the nullification of Stevin's process: from no wonder to wonder; a reintroduction of the puzzle, as opposed to its elimination. In producing an answer at a level even higher than the optimally resolved structure, this is precisely what the designer achieves.

TO use an expression from Donald Schön[31], instead of being a mere response, the new structure will recircumscribe or "reframe" the question; it will cause us to think again. Consequently, the new structure must go beyond the objective of stability, not so much contradicting as surpassing it; it must go beyond optimisation, to nurture the feeling of wonderment, and replace disillusionment with the enthusiasm evoked by Shaftesbury, Lessing's great mentor, with: "How wonderful a thing is the love of wondering and of raising wonder". The structures that promote this wonder are the structures that invite both learning and creativity.

STRUCTURES of this highest intelligence are related to constructive as well as destructive movement. As observed by Piaget, in their most intensive stage of learning, children appear to devote their energies to the destruction rather than the assembly of structures. They hurl objects and dismantle them. In so doing they begin to understand the world not as a static, closed object, but as a universe of open possibilities. And so it is with the structures of Santiago Calatrava: they manifest movement, rather than mask it. Not only do they succeed in standing; they do so in a way that is close to the optimal. Theirs is a cognitive achievement, at the highest level in the hierarchy of well-formed structures. Calatrava's structures keep that sense of wonder alive; they open the discerning eye; they are an open invitation to soaring and dream-work.

31. Donald Schön, *The Reflective Practitioner*, New York, Basic Books, 1983.

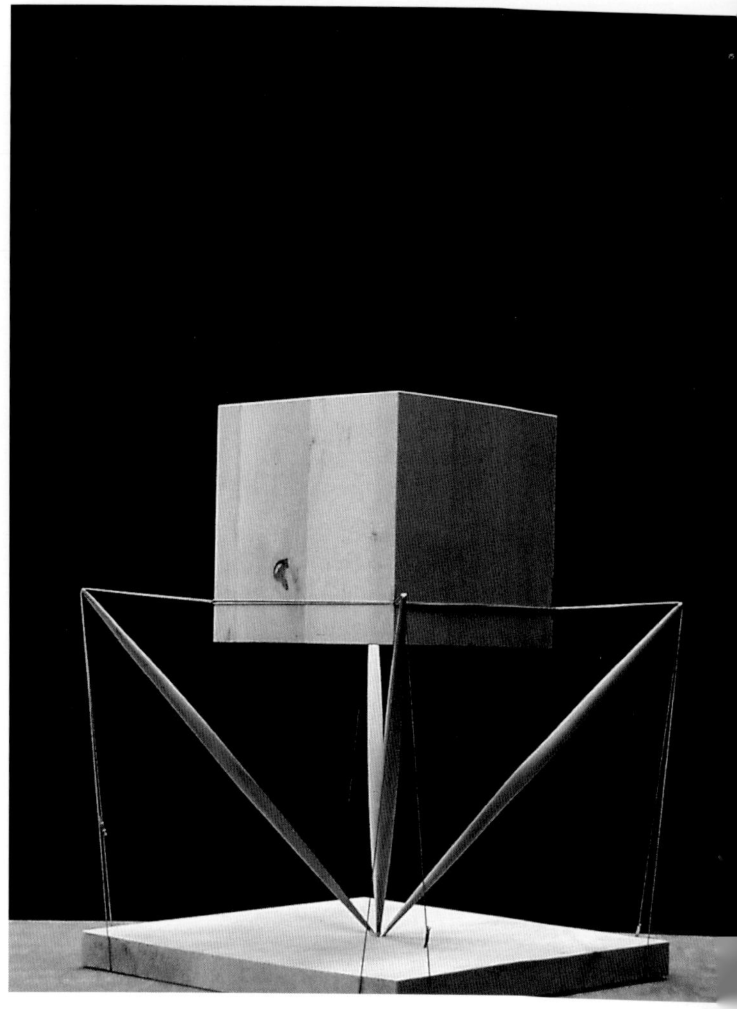

Calatrava sculptures

Pregnant Moment

Communication Tower Alicante. 1993.

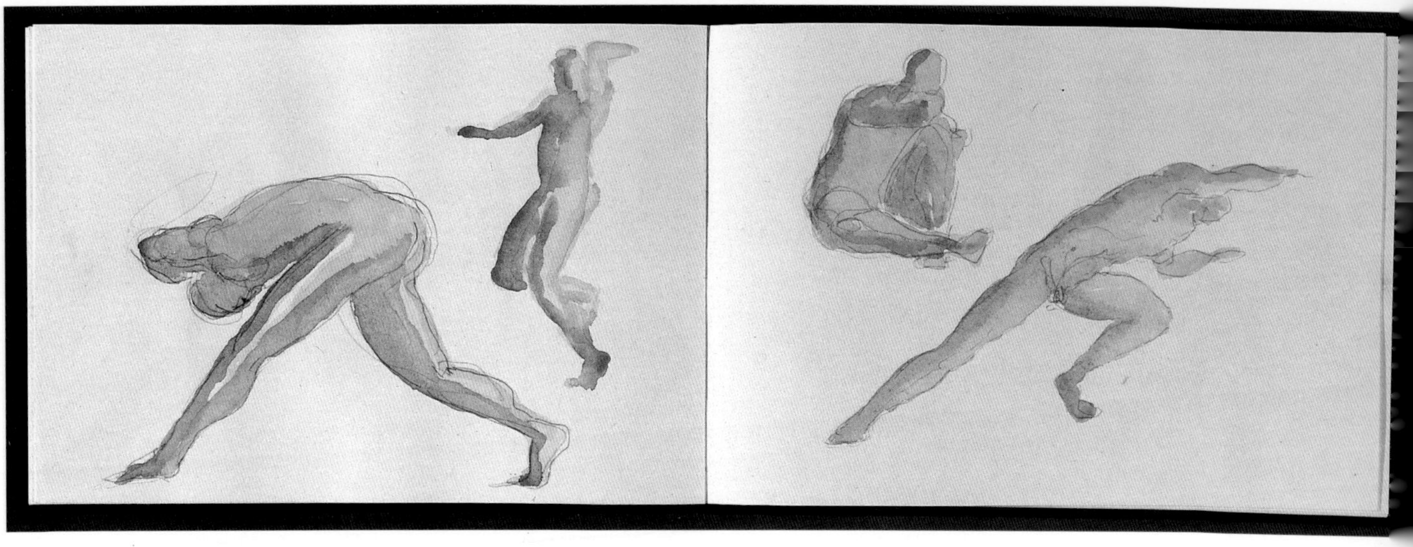

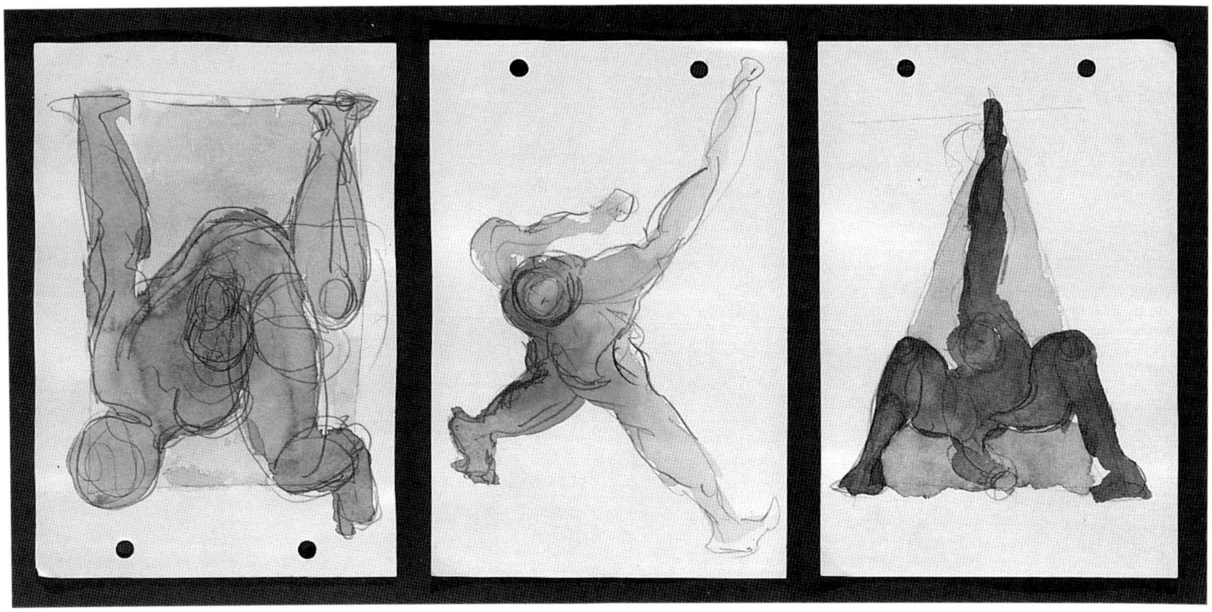

Calatrava. Human figure studies

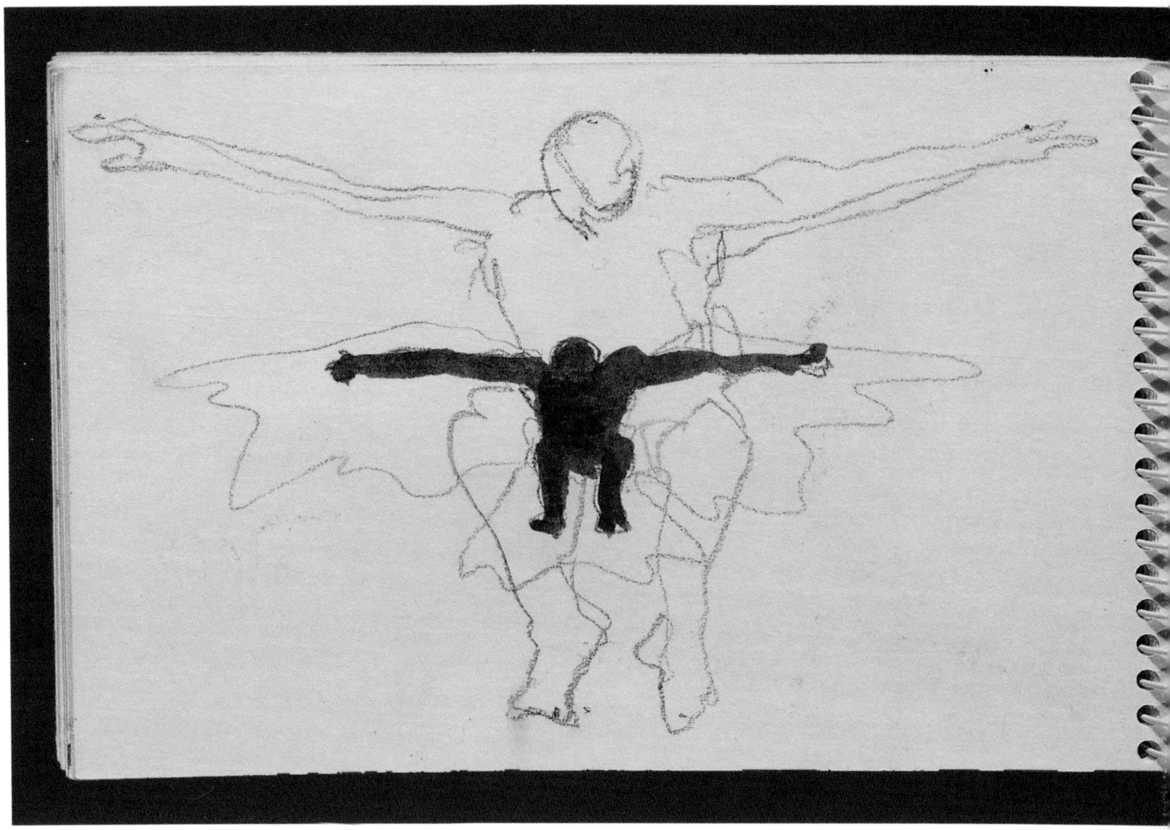

A COGNITIVE ACHIEVEMENT, AT THE HIGHEST LEVEL IN THE HIERARCHY OF WELL-FORMED STRUCTURES. CALATRAVA'S STRUCTURES KEEP THAT SENSE OF WONDER ALIVE; THEY OPEN THE DISCERNING EYE; THEY ARE AN OPEN INVITATION TO SOARING AND DREAM-WORK.

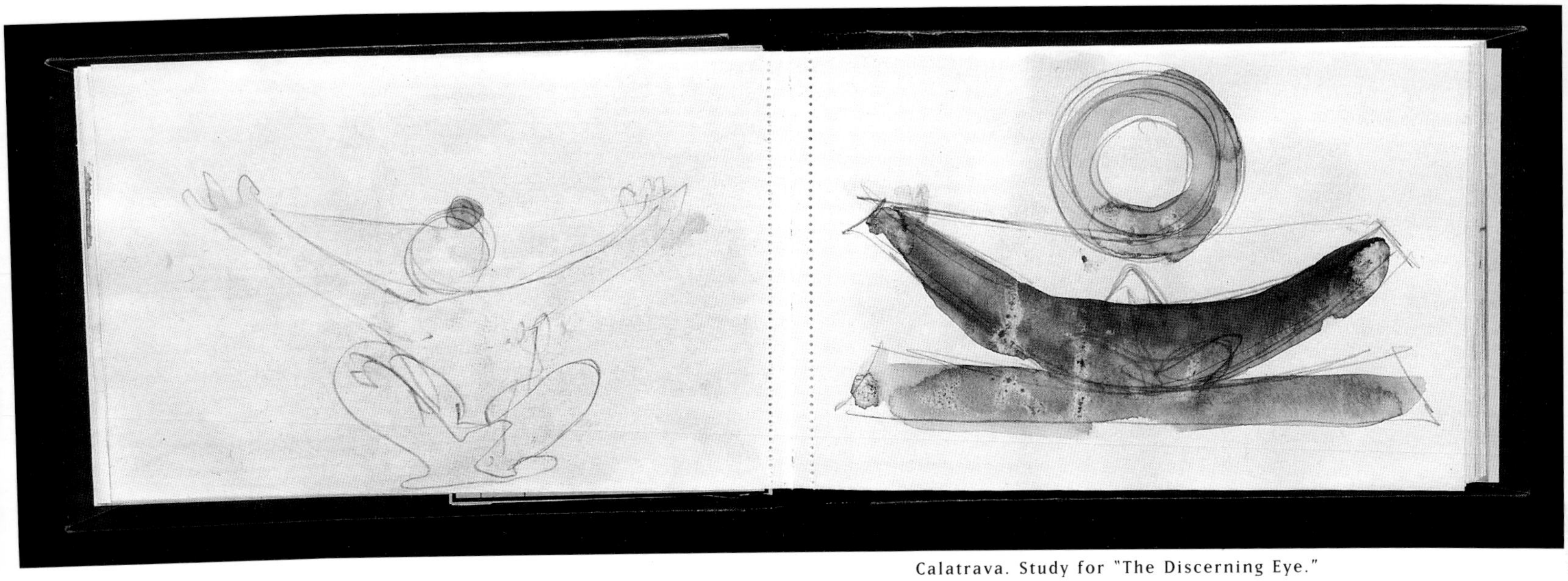

Calatrava. Study for "The Discerning Eye."

"The Discerning Eye."

APPENDIX

SOME EXCERPTS FROM THE
PH. D. DISSERTATION OF
SANTIAGO CALATRAVA,

ZUR FALTBARKEIT
VON FACHWERKEN
(ON THE FOLDABILITY OF FRAMES),
1981,

AT THE FEDERAL INSTITUTE
OF TECHNOLOGY (ETH) IN ZURICH
CONCERNING MOVEMENT
IN STRUCTURES.

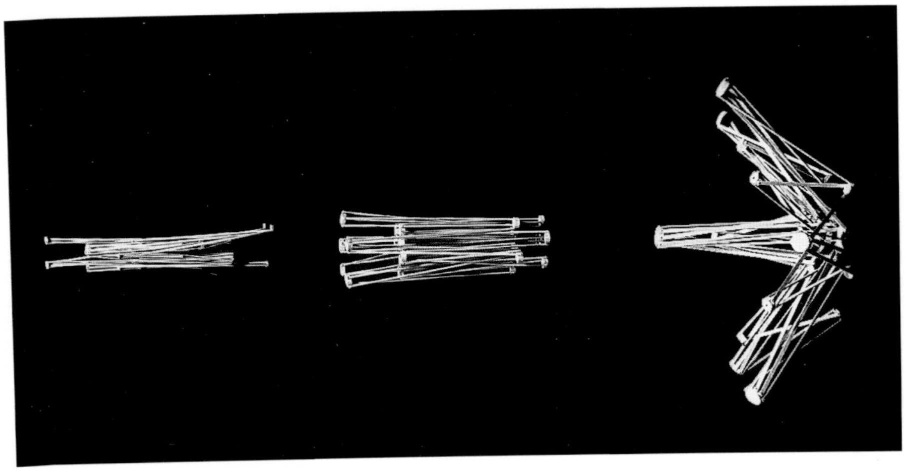

I

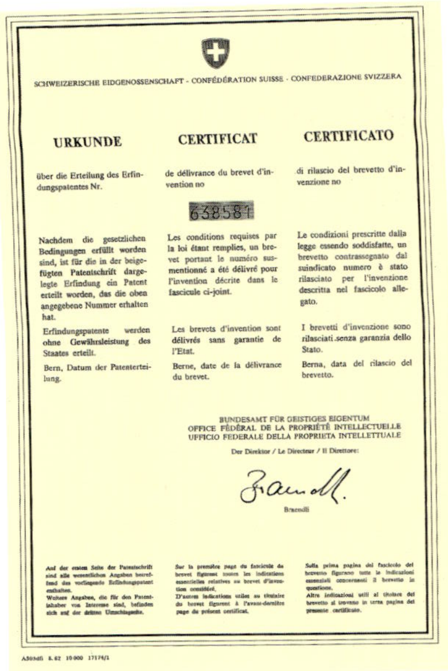

SCHWEIZERISCHE EIDGENOSSENSCHAFT · CONFÉDÉRATION SUISSE · CONFEDERAZIONE SVIZZERA

URKUNDE	CERTIFICAT	CERTIFICATO
über die Erteilung des Erfindungspatentes Nr.	de délivrance du brevet d'invention no	di rilascio del brevetto d'invenzione no
	638581	
Nachdem die gesetzlichen Bedingungen erfüllt worden sind, ist für die in der beigefügten Patentschrift dargelegte Erfindung ein Patent erteilt worden, das die oben angegebene Nummer erhalten hat.	Les conditions requises par la loi étant remplies, un brevet portant le numéro susmentionné a été délivré pour l'invention décrite dans le fascicule ci-joint.	Le condizioni prescritte dalla legge essendo soddisfatte, un brevetto contrassegnato dal suindicato numero è stato rilasciato per l'invenzione descritta nel fascicolo allegato.
Erfindungspatente werden ohne Gewährleistung des Staates erteilt.	Les brevets d'invention sont délivrés sans garantie de l'Etat.	I brevetti d'invenzione sono rilasciati senza garanzia dello Stato.
Bern, Datum der Patenterteilung.	Berne, date de la délivrance du brevet.	Berna, data del rilascio del brevetto.

BUNDESAMT FÜR GEISTIGES EIGENTUM
OFFICE FÉDÉRAL DE LA PROPRIÉTÉ INTELLECTUELLE
UFFICIO FEDERALE DELLA PROPRIETA INTELLETTUALE

Der Direktor / Le Directeur / Il Direttore:

Braendli

Auf der ersten Seite der Patentschrift sind alle wesentlichen Angaben betreffend das vorliegende Erfindungspatent enthalten. Weitere Angaben, die für den Patentinhaber von Interesse sind, befinden sich auf der dritten Umschlagseite.	Sur la première page du fascicule du brevet figurent toutes les indications essentielles relatives au brevet d'invention considéré. D'autres indications utiles au titulaire du brevet figurent à l'avant-dernière page du présent certificat.	Sulla prima pagina del fascicolo del brevetto figurano tutte le indicazioni essenziali concernenti il brevetto in questione. Altre indicazioni utili al titolare del brevetto si trovano in terza pagina del presente certificato.

A30sdfi 8.82 10000 17174/1

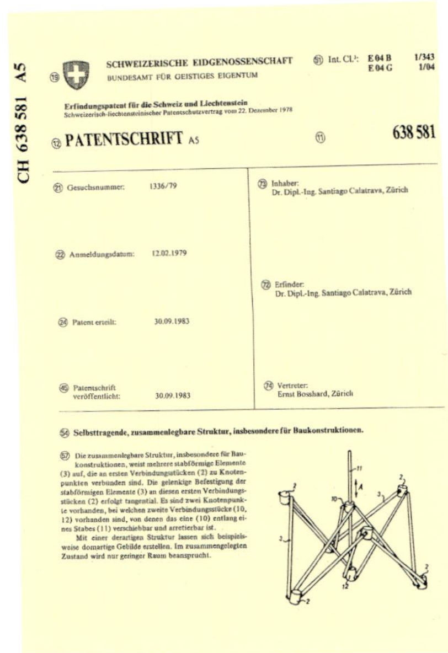

CH 638 581 A5

(19) SCHWEIZERISCHE EIDGENOSSENSCHAFT
BUNDESAMT FÜR GEISTIGES EIGENTUM

(51) Int. Cl.³: E 04 B 1/343; E 04 G 1/04

Erfindungspatent für die Schweiz und Liechtenstein
Schweizerisch-liechtensteinischer Patentschutzvertrag vom 22. Dezember 1978

(12) **PATENTSCHRIFT** A5

(11) 638 581

(21) Gesuchsnummer: 1336/79

(22) Anmeldungsdatum: 12.02.1979

(24) Patent erteilt: 30.09.1983

(45) Patentschrift veröffentlicht: 30.09.1983

(73) Inhaber: Dr. Dipl.-Ing. Santiago Calatrava, Zürich

(72) Erfinder: Dr. Dipl.-Ing. Santiago Calatrava, Zürich

(74) Vertreter: Ernst Bosshard, Zürich

(54) **Selbsttragende, zusammenlegbare Struktur, insbesondere für Baukonstruktionen.**

(57) Die zusammenlegbare Struktur, insbesondere für Baukonstruktionen, weist mehrere stabförmige Elemente (3) auf, die an ersten Verbindungsstücken (2) zu Knotenpunkten verbunden sind. Die gelenkige Befestigung der stabförmigen Elemente (3) an diesen ersten Verbindungsstücken (2) erfolgt tangential. Es sind zwei Knotenpunkte vorhanden, bei welchen zweite Verbindungsstücke (10, 12) vorhanden sind, von denen das eine (10) entlang eines Stabes (11) verschiebbar und arretierbar ist.

Mit einer derartigen Struktur lassen sich beispielsweise domartige Gebilde erstellen. Im zusammengelegten Zustand wird nur geringer Raum beansprucht.

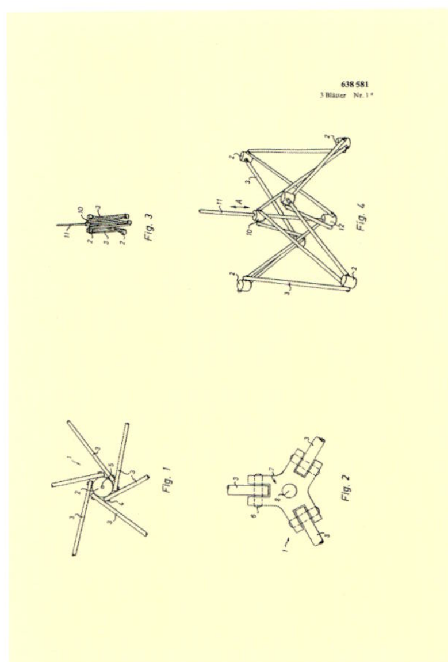

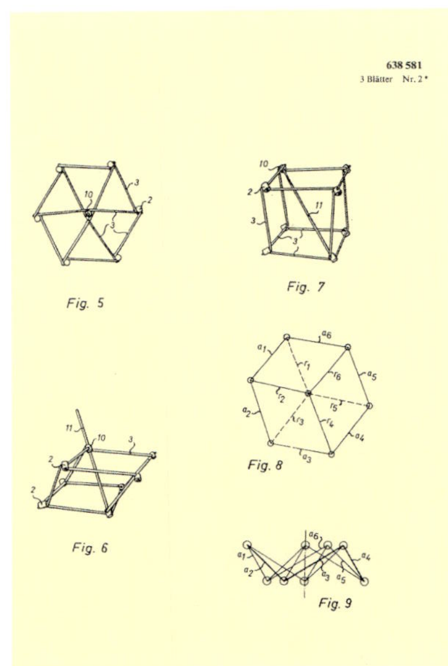

SWISS PATENT, 1983

DER KUBUS ALS GRUNDELEMENT DER FALTBARKEIT

Betrachten wir einen Kubus ABCDEFGH mit der Seitenlänge a, der Ecke A in der Ebene π und der Raumdiagonalen AH senkrecht zur Ebene π. Der Umriss der Projektion dieses Würfels auf die Ebene π bildet ein reguläres Sechseck.

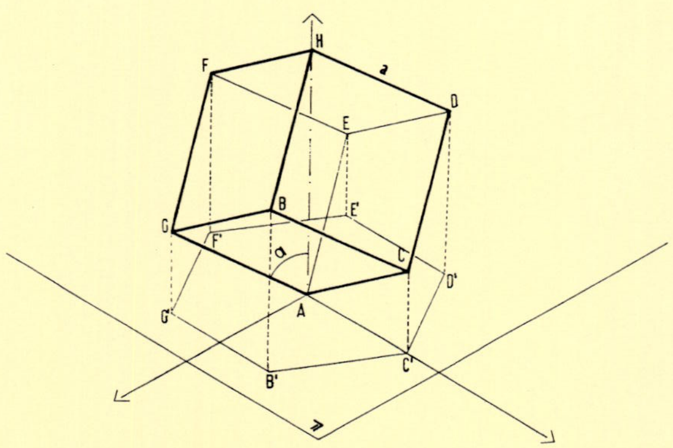

Ersetzen wir die Kanten des Polyeders durch Stäbe, die in den Ecken durch Gelenke verbunden sind. Die so entstandene Struktur hat folgenden Freiheitsgrad:

$$F = 3g - n - 6$$

g (Anzahl Knoten) = 6

n (Anzahl Stäbe) = 12

Es handelt sich um einen Mechanismus mit 6 Freiheitsgraden.

Transformation 1: Vom räumlichen zum ebenen Gebilde

Bewegen wir den Knoten H gegen A unter Einhaltung folgender geometrischer Bedingungen:

I Der Knoten H bewegt sich entlang der Raumdiagonalen AH gegen A.

II $\widehat{CAH} = \widehat{EAH} = \widehat{GAH} = \alpha$, wobei α entsprechend dem Abstand AH variiert.

Die eingeführten geometrischen Bedingungen bringen eine Beschränkung des Freiheitsgrades mit sich. Sie wirken sich wie folgt auf die kinematischen Bedingungen aus:

I $F' = -2$

II $F' = -3$

Der gesamte Freiheitsgrad ist:

$$F = 6 - 2 - 3 = 1$$

Der Mechanismus wird zwangsläufig; damit ergibt sich folgende Abhängigkeit vom Parameter α:

$$\overline{AH} = 3\,a\cos\alpha$$
$$\overline{BB'} = \overline{DD'} = \overline{FF'} = 2\,a\cos\alpha$$
$$\overline{CC'} = \overline{EE'} = \overline{GG'} = a\cos\alpha$$
$$\overline{AB'} = \overline{AC'} = \overline{AD'} = \overline{AE'} = \overline{AF'} = \overline{AG'} = a\sin\alpha$$
$$\overline{B'C'} = \overline{C'D'} = \overline{D'E'} = \overline{E'F'} = \overline{F'G'} = \overline{G'B'} = a\sin\alpha$$

Das bedeutet, dass der Umriss der Projektion der Knoten B, C, D, E, F, G auf die Ebene π ein reguläres Sechseck mit Seitenlänge $a' = a\sin\alpha$ und Zentrum in A ergibt.

Durch Aenderung des Parameters α erhält man folgende numerische Werte für die Längen $\overline{AB'}$, $\overline{BB'}$, $\overline{CC'}$ und HA:

α	0°	35.2643°	54.7355°	90°
$\overline{AB'}$	0	0.5773 a	0.8160 a	a
$\overline{CC'}$	a	0.8160 a	0.5773 a	0
$\overline{BB'}$	2 a	1.6329 a	1.1547 a	0
HA	3 a	2.4494 a	1.7320 a	0

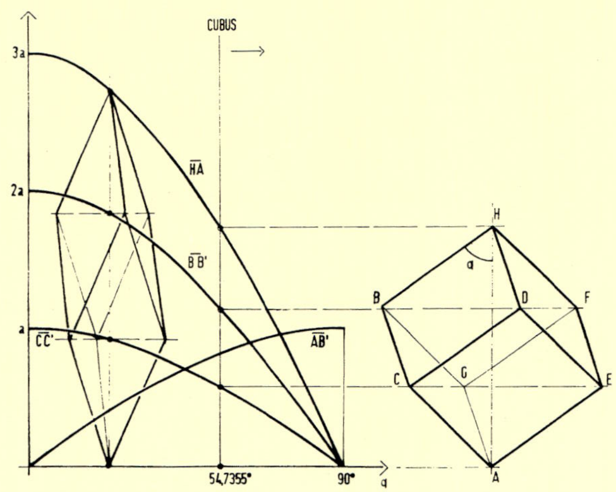

Für α = 0, $\overline{AB'}$ = 0, $\overline{BB'}$ = a, $\overline{CC'}$ = 2a, $\overline{HA}$ = 3a, d.h. es liegen alle Stäbe der ursprünglichen Struktur parallel um ein Segment mit der Länge 3a gruppiert.

Für α = 90°, $\overline{AB'}$ = a, $\overline{AB'}$ = $\overline{BB'}$ = $\overline{CC'}$ = $\overline{HA}$ = 0, d.h. es liegen alle Stäbe der Struktur auf der Ebene π; der ursprüngliche Kubus ist in ein reguläres Sechseck mit Seite a, den Ecken B,C,D,E,F,G und Zentrum in den zwei übereinanderliegenden Punkten A und H übergegangen.

Die folgende Photoserie zeigt den oben beschriebenen Faltvorgang am Modell:

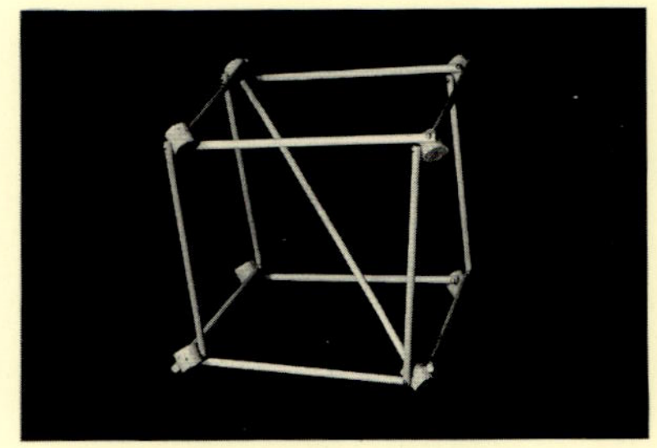

Bild 1:

Die Struktur in ihrer Ausgangslage

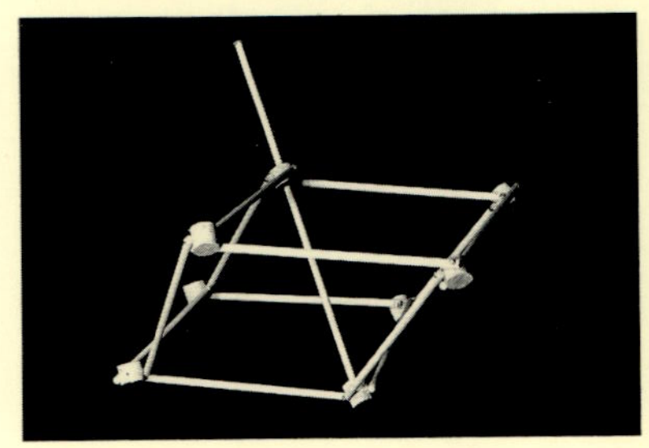

Bild 2:

Verschiebung des Knotens H entlang der Raumdiagonalen AH in Richtung A

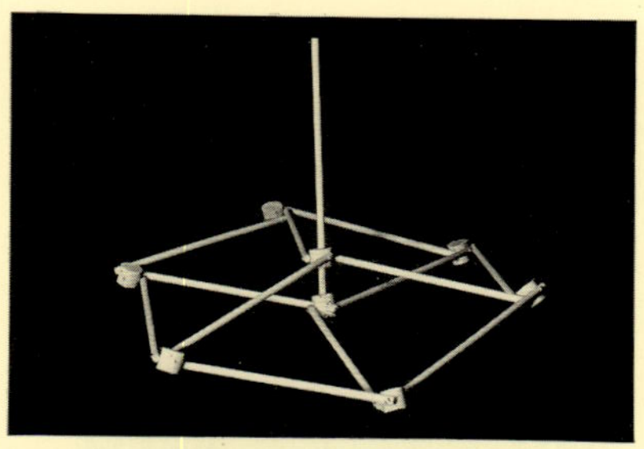

Bild 3

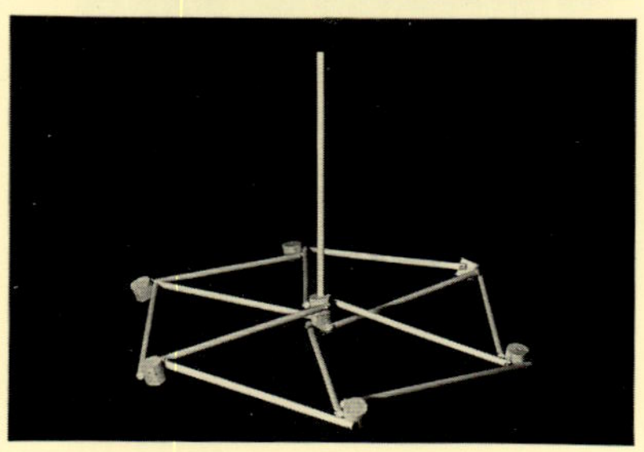

Bild 4:

Die Stäbe des Würfels sowie der Knoten H zusammen mit dem Knoten A kommen in die Ebene π zu liegen und bilden dort ein reguläres Sechseck

Transformation 2: Vom ebenen zum linearen Gebilde

Indem wir von der Position ausgehen, bei der alle Stäbe des ursprünglichen Kubus auf der Ebene π liegen, können wir eine Transformation ausführen, die folgende Bedingungen erfüllt:

1. Der Knoten A bleibt fest in der Ebene π.
2. Die Knoten B, D und F bleiben in der Ebene π verschiebbar.
3. Der Knoten H entfernt sich von A entlang der Raumdiagonalen des ursprünglichen Kubus.

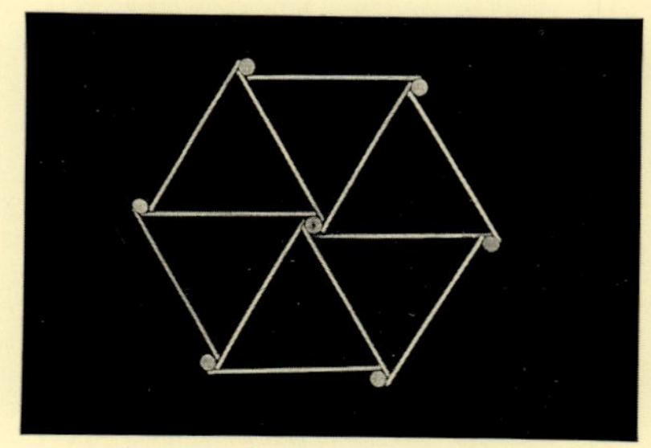

Ausgangslage der Transformation 2. Alle Knoten liegen auf der Ebene π. Die Stäbe bilden ein Sechseck mit seinen Radien

Die geometrischen Bedingungen II) und III) wirken sich auf die kinematischen Bedingungen aus, indem sie den Freiheitsgrad des Mechanismus wie folgt beschränken:

II $F' = -3$

III $F' = -2$

Der gesamte Freiheitsgrad (ursprünglich $F = 6$) wird zu:

$$F = 6 - 3 - 2 = 1$$

Der Mechanismus ist zwangsläufig.

So ergibt sich folgende Abhängigkeit vom Parameter α:

$$\overline{AH} = \overline{CC'} = \overline{EE'} = \overline{GG'} = a\cos\alpha$$

$$\overline{AB} = \overline{AC'} = \overline{AD} = \overline{AF'} = \overline{AF} = \overline{AG'} = a\sin\alpha$$

$$\overline{BC'} = \overline{C'D} = \overline{DE'} = \overline{E'F} = \overline{FG'} = \overline{G'B} = a\sin\alpha$$

Das heisst, der Umriss der Projektion der Knoten B, C, D, E, F, G auf die Ebene π ergibt ein reguläres Sechseck mit der Seitenlänge $a' = a$ und dem Zentrum in A.

Graphische Darstellung:

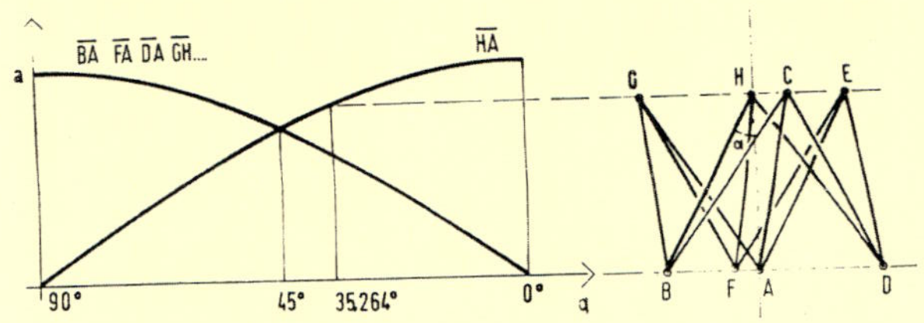

Für α = 35.2643° entsprechen die Punkte B, C, D, E, F, G den Ecken eines Oktaeders mit der Seite a.

Für α = 0° sind die Distanzen $\overline{HC}$, $\overline{HE}$, $\overline{HG}$ sowie auch $\overline{AB}$, $\overline{AD}$, $\overline{AF}$ gleich 0, und die Stäbe AC, AE, AG usw. liegen um eine Achse senkrecht zur Ebene π.

Die folgende Photoserie zeigt den oben beschriebenen Faltvorgang am Modell:

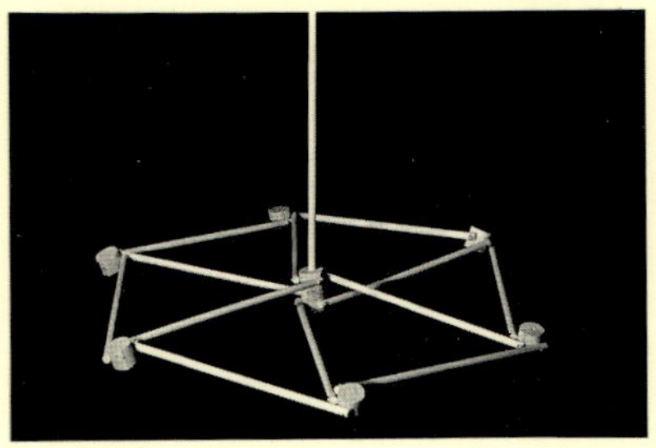

Bild 1:

Alle Stäbe und Knoten liegen auf der Ebene π.

α = 90°

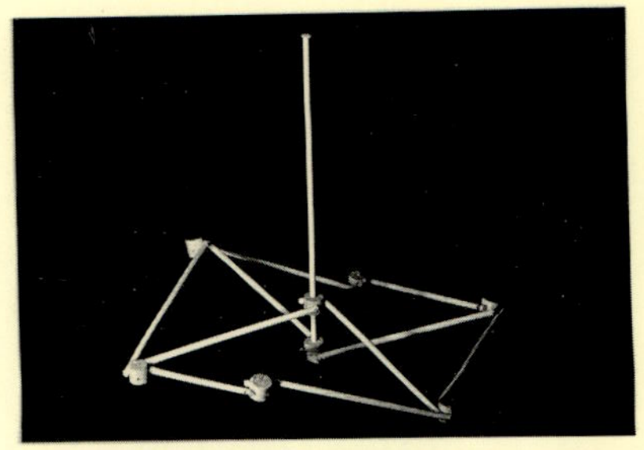

Bild 2:

Die Knoten H, B, C und D entfernen sich von der Ebene π.

α ≃ 70°

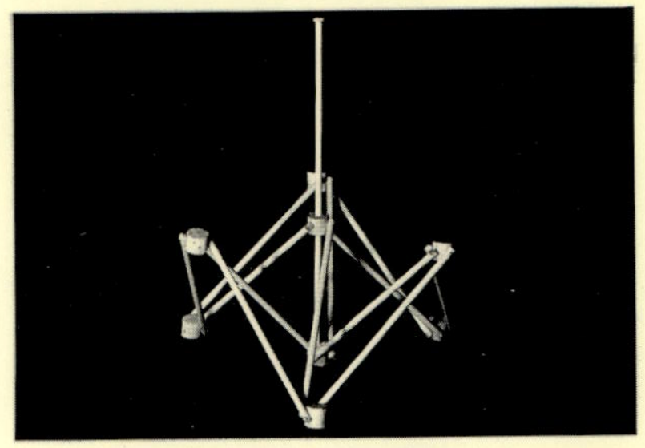

Bild 3:

α ≃ 45°

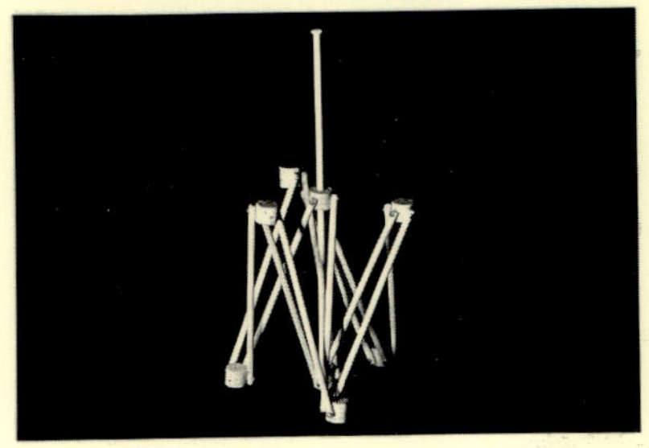

Bild 4:

α ≃ 25°

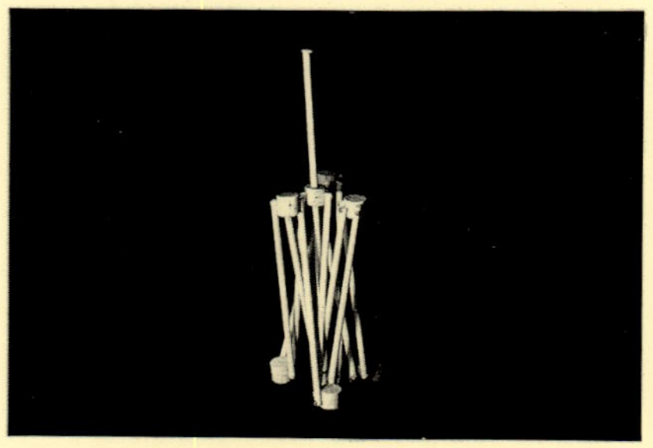

<u>Bild 5:</u>

$\alpha \simeq 0^\circ$

Halten wir fest:

1. Das ursprünglich <u>räumliche</u> Modulare Grundelement lässt sich durch eine räumliche Transformation in ein <u>ebenes</u>, und durch eine weitere räumliche Transformation in ein <u>lineares</u> Element umwandeln.

2. Während des ganzen Faltungsprozesses bildet die Projektion des Grundelementes auf die Ebene π unter Beibehaltung gewisser geometrischer Bedingungen immer ein reguläres Sechseck.

<u>Darstellung der ummantelnden Flächen in der zweiten Phase des Faltvorgangs (vom ebenen zum linearen Gebilde):</u>

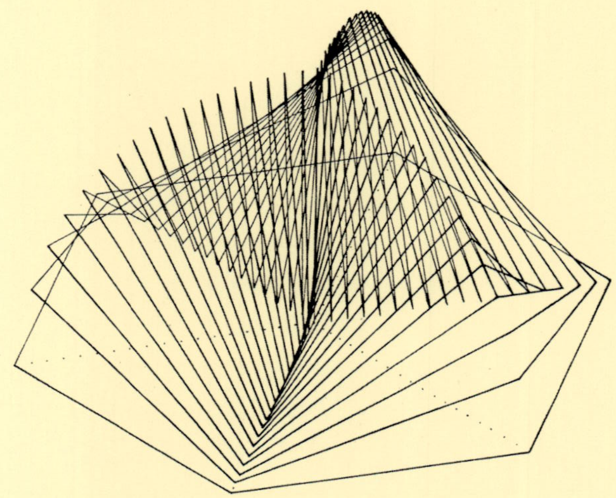

Die folgende Photosequenz zeigt den geordneten Vorgang der Verschiebung von Knoten und Stäben vom gefalteten Zustand bis zur vollständigen Entfaltung der Struktur in Seitensicht.

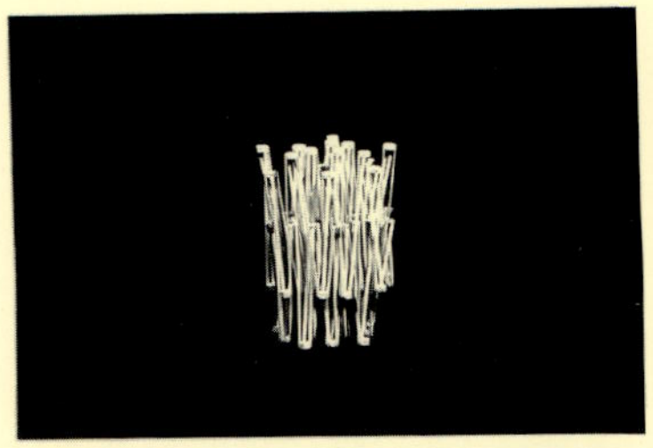

Bild 1:

Alle Stäbe und Knoten sind um eine gemeinsame Achse gruppiert.

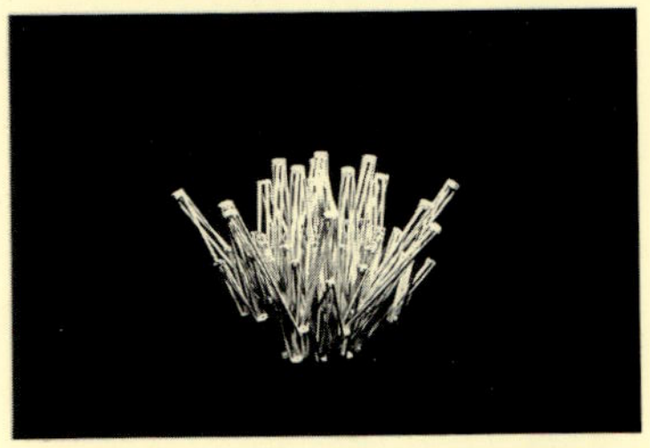

Bild 2:

Die oberen Knoten entfernen sich radial von der gemeinsamen Achse.

Bild 3:

Zwischenstadium der Entfaltung.

Bild 4:

Zwischenstadium der Entfaltung.

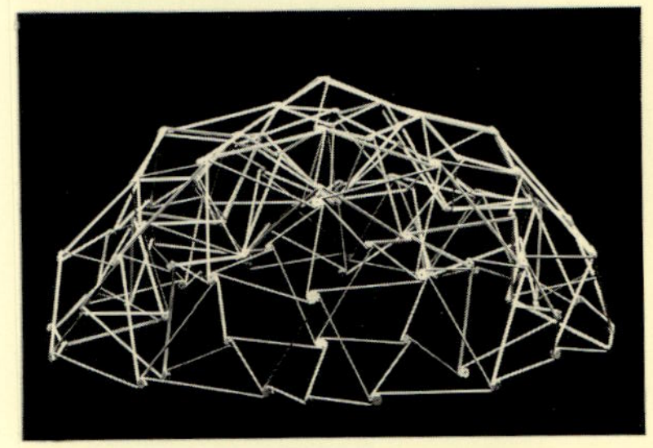

Bild 5:

Die unteren Knoten entfernen sich radial von ihrer ursprünglichen Lage.

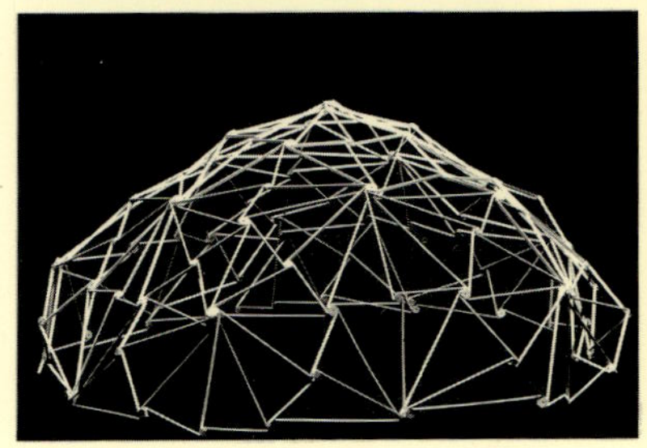

Bild 6:

Die vollständig entfaltete Struktur. Die zur Entfaltung der Struktur gelösten Bindungen werden wieder fixiert.